For Ginny, Emily, and Dan

THE EDGE OF MALICE

The Marie Grossman Story

David P. Miraldi

 Prometheus Books

Guilford, Connecticut

 Prometheus Books

An imprint of The Rowman & Littlefield Publishing Group, Inc.
4501 Forbes Boulevard, Suite 200
Lanham, Maryland 20706
www.rowman.com

Distributed by NATIONAL BOOK NETWORK

British Library Cataloguing in Publication Information Available

Library of Congress Control Number: 2019955299

∞™ The paper used in this publication meets the minimum requirements of American National Standard for Information Sciences Permanence of Paper for Printed Library Materials, ANSI/NISO Z39.48-1992.

CONTENTS

PREFACE

During the course of an attorney's career, there are usually a handful of cases that stand out as the most memorable. And from that select group, there is usually one that sits atop of the list. For me, that one case involved Marie Grossman. I knew and admired Marie before the events described in this book ever happened. Since then, my respect for her has only grown. It was an honor when she allowed me to tell her story.

This book is one of creative nonfiction. Like other works in this genre, the events described in this book are true, but the dialogues and thoughts of the characters have been re-created. In order to protect their privacy, I have also changed the names of several people involved in the story.

With those few explanations out of the way, I hope that you will find as much inspiration in Marie's story as I have.

Part I

The Crime

I

COLLISION COURSE

Disoriented and groggy, Richard Thompson rolled over on the bare mattress that elevated him a few inches above the worn carpet. His tall body rested diagonally across the mattress, one leg dangling over its edge like an oar poised above the water's surface. The room was cold despite the periodic firing of an electric heater whose orange filaments made more noise than heat. During the night, someone had thrown a red plaid blanket over him, and he hugged its rumpled mass to his chest.

At first, he wasn't sure where he was. Cardboard covered the room's one broken window and diffuse light peeked from its periphery, giving Richard just enough illumination to identify the shapes of the furniture. He squeezed his eyes shut while shaking his head, hoping that this combination would jump-start his brain. He raised his head and instantly felt woozy. When the dizziness had passed, he realized that he was in Christopher's apartment and it was morning.

He and Christopher Martin had gotten high the night before—something they'd been doing regularly for the past six months. Although his family's home was just a few blocks away, he'd decided not to walk back there last night. Sure, it had been cold—December nights in Cleveland usually were—but he'd been wasted. Stoned and alone, he'd have been an easy target for one of the gangs that roamed his neighborhood. Hough could be a dangerous place at any hour of the day, but after midnight, it was no place for someone to take a stroll—gun or no gun.

Last night's weed had been strong—laced with hash, if you believed Christopher, but who knew? Christopher was a bullshit artist and not to be trusted; yet, time and again, Richard cast his lot with him.

They were both nineteen and had known each other since grade school. Neither had a regular job; when they needed money, they robbed—except they never called it that. For them, it was going out and "making" money. Richard had branched out a little by selling weed, but he was a small-timer, the last link in a chain of suppliers and middlemen.

Christopher was short, stocky, and muscular. His constant sneer warned of a latent anger that could surface quickly. Christopher was fearless and without conscience, qualities that made him an able partner. As a kid, he'd struggled in school and disrupted the classroom, leading to several suspensions and his inevitable dropping out. After that, he'd survived by his cunning on the street.

Richard had come to crime by a different route. Unlike Christopher, he had been raised in a stable family. His parents, both industrious people from Louisiana, had migrated to Cleveland seeking better-paying jobs in the 1960s. His mother was a faithful Baptist who took him to church every Sunday until, as a teenager, he'd refused to go anymore. His father was also a strong presence, working a variety of jobs and coaching youth basketball teams in his free time. Despite their hard work, they were still living in Hough and struggling to pay their bills. Young guys working the street had more to show for their efforts than his parents, an irony not lost on Richard.

His future had initially looked bright. He had been a high school basketball star and had been offered a full athletic scholarship to Purdue. However, his basketball skills had been both a blessing and a curse. His high school teachers didn't require him to do much of anything; they'd pass him in order to maintain his athletic eligibility. Although the world had its rules, Richard soon believed that they didn't apply to him. In the end, one teacher had given him a failing mark in a civics course and he hadn't graduated with his class. Although he'd made up the class in summer school and received his diploma, his scholarship had been yanked, with little hope of a future reinstatement. To compound things, he'd gotten his girlfriend pregnant and he was now the father of a baby girl.

Then there were the drugs. It all started by hanging out with the wrong guys. He had begun using pot and coke in high school, sometimes getting high before basketball games. After he left school, his drug use had steadily increased until it dominated his life. He wasn't exactly sure when that had happened, only that it had. He now lived to get high and would do whatever he needed to support his habit.

Today would be like any other. He and Christopher would smoke the rest of their weed and then buy more. They were both broke, which meant that they would eventually have to "make" some money. They were good at that.

* * *

Twelve miles away in Lakewood, Ohio, Marie Grossman was beginning a day that promised to be busy. The forty-five-year-old wife and mother of two was scheduled to spend her entire workday in meetings at the Cleveland Clinic. After that, she would rush directly to Hawken School, where her younger son would be wrestling in a high school meet. She had risen around 7 a.m., showered, and dressed in a rust-colored business suit. By 8 a.m., she was backing her blue, two-door Mustang onto Lake Road for the drive to the Clinic.

As daylight began to push away the darkness, a morning fog reduced visibility to less than two blocks. She assumed that once it burned off, the weather would revert to what Clevelanders came to expect in December—gray overcast skies with temperatures hovering around freezing. Usually, the only variable was the amount of wind and rain. Today, temperatures were predicted to rise into the upper forties.

Traffic was heavy by the time she merged onto the Shoreway. Focusing on the bumper-to-bumper traffic, she sporadically listened to the morning news broadcast for this Friday, December 11, 1987. President Reagan and Mikhail Gorbachev had just concluded a three-day summit aimed at limiting strategic weapons. She slammed on her brakes as a red Ford Fiesta cut into her lane, its driver talking animatedly with his passenger. Her right hand was poised over the horn, ready to bear down on it, but the danger had passed and she gave the careless driver a free pass.

When the news ended, she clicked off the radio to focus on her upcoming meetings at the Clinic. Since July, she'd been working for

Preferred Healthcare, a company that was setting up mental health networks in various cities for businesses that ran their own employee health plans. Today she and a fellow employee, John Wellston, were meeting with psychiatrists, nonphysician psychiatric staff, and administrators to determine what services the Cleveland Clinic could provide. They would quiz the Clinic staff about not only the quality of its care but also its controls in eliminating unnecessary psychiatric treatment.

The sprawling Cleveland Clinic campus was located in Cleveland's run-down Hough and Fairfax neighborhoods, two of the city's highest-crime areas. To keep its employees and patients safe, the Clinic employed a security force that was the second largest in Cuyahoga County, bested in numbers only by Cleveland's own police department. After parking in one of the Clinic's parking garages, she walked briskly to the main building and met her colleague in the central lobby.

After exchanging pleasantries, she and John met with the head of the Clinic's psychiatric department, their first appointment. The morning meetings spilled one into the next, leaving just enough time to grab a salad for lunch at the hospital's cafeteria. The afternoon sessions followed much the same pattern. As they finished up their last appointment, Marie glanced at her watch and saw that it was 5:30 p.m. Although Wellston's face showed exhaustion, he still wanted to talk about the day's meetings.

"Do you have time for a coffee?" he asked.

"No coffee for me, but I can talk for ten minutes or so. I need to get to my son's wrestling match." Pointing to an empty waiting area near the psychiatry check-in desk, she said, "Let's just sit here for a few minutes."

They found two chairs positioned at a ninety-degree angle to one another, sat down, and began reviewing their notes. Instead of asking specific questions and giving a general overview, Wellston discussed each meeting, highlighting the major points and identifying what they still needed to do for follow-up. Marie checked her watch again. It was 6:05.

"John, I really need to wrap this up," she said.

"Okay. Just a couple more things. I would like you to follow up with the numbers guy; I can't remember his name."

"You mean Silverton. I will and I'll call you after I do."

"Great. Do you need me to walk you out to your car?"

"No, that's all right. It's in the parking garage. Should still be lots of people there now."

✿ ✿ ✿

Richard Thompson and Christopher Martin drove over to Richard's house in the late morning of Friday, December 11. By now, both of Richard's parents were at work and his two younger sisters were at school. He had some pot stashed there, and they smoked it in the living room while watching television on a small black-and-white set. By 2:30 p.m., they were back at Christopher's place, where they shared a few joints with Christopher's girlfriend until they had smoked the last of his supply. At 4:30 p.m., Christopher told his girlfriend that they needed to go out and "make" some money.

They piled into Richard's blue Chevy. As Richard started his car, he said, "I feel like Burger King again. That okay with you?"

"Yeah, my car's broken down in the Burger King lot. I gotta check on it anyway."

Richard nodded and felt for the .38-caliber revolver in his left jacket pocket.

Over the past three months, the two had committed fifteen robberies at nearby fast-food restaurants following a plan that Christopher had devised. They would drive to one of the area's restaurants, park in the back lot, and remain in the car until the right opportunity presented itself. When the drive-thru line had just one customer, a lone woman, they would make their move. Because the woman would lower the car's window to place her order, it was easy for Richard or Christopher to stick a gun through it and point it at the woman's head. Whispering or gesturing, they'd tell her to unlock all of the doors and let them in. Once in, they'd direct her to drive to an ATM and withdraw her maximum cash limit. After she'd handed the money over to them, they'd force her out of the car and take off in it.

Only six weeks earlier, the two had robbed a young woman at the drive-thru at this same Burger King. Located on Euclid Avenue, it occupied the entire frontage between East Eighty-Fifth Street and East Eighty-Sixth Street. The parking lot was not fenced, nor was there much illumination in the back. Although the building's rear had a solid door at one corner, it had no windows. The drive-thru menu board was located about fifteen yards from the back of the building, almost direct-ly even with the rear door. Employees or patrons inside the building could not view the back lot or the menu board. Except for several three-story apartment buildings bordering the back lot, it was secluded.

"You think they've added a video camera since last time?" Christo-pher asked.

"I went by there yesterday and there wasn't one then," Richard said. "We'll look again."

They reached the restaurant around 4:45, just as the sun began to set in the heavily overcast skies. They parked in the rear, and Richard got out to look around. When he got back into the car, he told Christopher that he didn't see any surveillance cameras. He'd also peeked into the restaurant's front window to check for a security guard—no security guard and just a few patrons inside the restaurant.

Over the next hour and a half, they watched as about fifty customers used the drive-thru. They'd seen plenty of cars with men in them and about a dozen with passengers, but none with just a lone woman and no other vehicles behind her. Around 6:20, there was a lull in the drive-thru traffic. A blue Mustang turned off of Euclid Avenue and slowly made its way toward the drive-thru order board. The Mustang's sole occupant was a woman. Both men got out of the car.

* * *

In order to reach Hawken School in time for her son's match, Marie knew that she had only thirty to forty-five minutes. Her son Joe wres-tled at one of the lower weight classes and was usually the second or third match. She considered driving straight there, but she had not eaten much for lunch and she was hungry. If she hustled, she could buy some fast food and get there in time. Although she had never stopped at the Burger King at Euclid and East Eighty-Fifth Street, she knew it was there. She had driven by it many times on her way to University Circle, a few blocks farther to the east.

After passing a turreted Victorian limestone church at East Eighty-Sixth, she came to the Burger King restaurant. As her Mustang pulled into the front parking lot, Marie caught a glimpse of the restaurant's interior—no patrons inside as far as she could tell. She smiled, con-vinced her order would be filled quickly. As she drove behind the building, she spotted the menu board to her left. She was in luck again—no one ahead of her.

Just a few seconds after Marie stopped, a female voice came from the menu board and asked her if she was ready to order. Marie lowered her window.

"I would like an order of six chicken tenders," she said. As she was considering her drink choice, a man suddenly slipped between the menu board and her car. She had no idea where he'd come from. Just as quickly, he pointed a revolver through her open window, not more than six inches from her temple. With his left hand, he held a finger to his lips—the universal sign to remain quiet.

She could see that he was a dark-skinned African American male, very tall and thin, probably in his early twenties. He had not bothered to use a mask to cover his long face. In the dim light, she saw his short-cropped hair and a day's growth of stubble. His eyes were deeply blood-shot, and despite the forty-degree weather, she saw perspiration on his forehead.

The gun made it hard for her to think. *You're being robbed. Give him your purse,* she reasoned. That's what experts always said to do in this situation—just hand over your money and credit cards. Don't hesitate. Just do it. Her purse was located in the middle console near the gear shift. She slowly reached for it, picked it up, and held it by the open window.

"Here is my purse," she said, hoping that the employee taking her order would hear her.

She placed her purse on the ledge of the car's open window and released her grip. It dropped to the pavement below, where some of its contents spilled onto the cold black asphalt. The man made no effort to take any of it. He gestured and looked across the car, apparently making eye contact with someone else. Without taking her eyes off of the man with the gun, Marie realized that her assailant had an accomplice. The man with the gun was reaching inside her car with his free hand. What did he want?

"Do you want my car?" Marie asked, again hoping that the Burger King employee would hear her and send help. Demonstrating that she needed to shut up, the man glared at her and held his finger to his lips again.

The man used his left hand to open the driver's-side door and then quickly slipped it behind her seat, pushing it forward as he attempted to force his way into the backseat. They wanted to get in. That was clear.

Although she was extremely frightened, Marie's mind worked rapidly and logically. *They don't want my money and they don't want my car. My God, they want me. I'm going to be raped*, she concluded. She revolted at the thought. She knew rape—the violence, the ugliness, and the shame. Once summoned, its memory was both vivid and acrid. No, she would not be raped again. Of that much she was sure.

The gun was inches from her head. The man with bloodshot eyes could shoot her if she didn't follow his instructions. She closed her eyes for a brief second. Her hands squeezed the steering wheel, choking it in a death grip. She knew the risk, but the next move would be hers. Whatever happened to her tonight would happen right here, right now, in the Burger King parking lot.

2

BEFORE

Anyone familiar with Marie Grossman's past would not have been surprised by how she ultimately chose to respond to the armed man confronting her. She had inherited a keen intelligence and resourcefulness from both her mother and father. Throughout her life, she had sought new challenges and opportunities. She was attracted by jobs that stretched her current abilities and forced her to master new skills. After a job became routine, she hungered for something new. For Marie, life was always about the next big adventure.

One only had to look to Marie's parents to find the roots of her personality. She was the older of two daughters born to Walter Joseph "Joe" Choborda and Miriam Snyder Choborda. Both parents came from poor but stable families, and each was the first in their family to graduate from college. They both knew how to overcome serious obstacles and carve out better lives for themselves.

Marie's father was one of eight children born to Slovakian immigrants who'd settled in Newark, New Jersey. Joe was the fourth oldest and was the second oldest of four boys born in rapid succession, each about a year apart. As youngsters, the four slept crossways in one bed. Because they shared the same clothes, the earliest to rise grabbed the best clothing. During the Great Depression, Joe dropped out of school in the eighth grade and landed a job in a foundry to help with family expenses.

One day he spotted men in suits touring the plant. He asked someone, "Hey, how do I get to be like them?"

One of the workers replied, "Those are college men. You gotta go to college if you want a job like that."

Without telling his mother, Joe returned to high school. His brothers made up the difference in his lost earnings, and Joe graduated from Irvington High School in three years.

The brothers were all outstanding athletes and played semiprofessional football as teenagers. Joe was the quarterback of a team that featured three of his brothers in the backfield. Joe's athletic ability caught the eye of a recruiter from Colgate University, and an athletic scholarship soon followed. When he arrived by bus in Hamilton, New York, he did not have the money to pay for the taxi drive to campus. Instead, with his suitcase in hand, he hitchhiked the remaining few miles.

Somehow navigating a world of privilege of which he was not a member, Joe earned his degree while playing both baseball and football for Colgate. After graduation, he entered a management training program at the American Can Company, where he started as a foreman at its Jersey City factory. While taking a weekend break at the Jersey Shore, he met his future wife, Miriam Snyder.

Widowed in her early thirties, Miriam's mother fended for herself and three children. She opened her three-bedroom house to boarders, students at the nearby Western Union School. To supplement that income, she used her dining room to host bridge parties and stocked the hall bookshelves with small gifts, greeting cards, and wrapping paper. Anyone who needed a birthday gift could come, pick it out, and have it gift-wrapped in a jiffy. She maintained a large vegetable garden and canned much of the harvest for year-round use. A strong woman of faith, she rarely missed church and visited the sick frequently.

Miriam was a gifted pianist and excellent student, graduating from high school at sixteen. Her mother found the means to send her to the New Jersey State Teachers College at Trenton, where she graduated with a degree in elementary school education. Miriam's first teaching position was at a one-room schoolhouse with multiple grades. As a young teacher, she found it difficult to maintain discipline in this mixed-age environment and sought other employment after two years. She was working as a clerk at a Hahne's department store when she met Joe Choborda.

After they were married, they moved into a working-class neighborhood in Irvington, New Jersey, a step above the rough neighborhoods of Newark. Their first child, Marie, was born on February 15, 1942, and another daughter followed a year and a half later. The girls shared a bedroom in a two-bedroom flat until the family moved to a slightly better neighborhood in Garwood, New Jersey. Joe was moving up the ladder at American Can, and their house in Garwood reflected that slight shift in their fortunes.

Marie was raised in a stable, loving environment and thrived. Like her parents, Marie was an excellent student. Although her mother could not interest her in music, Marie enjoyed art, particularly drawing. She delighted in the summer evenings when she and a hodgepodge of neighborhood kids played spud, a street dodgeball game that often lasted until the streetlights came on.

Although not excited by the prospect, Marie joined the Girl Scouts at her mother's bidding. To her surprise, she quickly came to love camping and the outdoors. By the time she was in junior high, she relished her two weeks at scout camp, which culminated in a canoe trip down the Delaware River. At day's end, the girls pulled their canoes from the river, cooked their supper, and slept under the stars.

Marie attended a regional high school that drew students from six adjoining towns, including Garwood and Berkeley Heights, where Bell Labs was located. For the first time, Marie interacted with children from higher income levels who had different post–high school aspirations. Through them, she realized that women did not have to become secretaries, teachers, or nurses.

In high school, she excelled in academics and was surrounded by a small, close-knit group of friends. Friday night football games were especially fun. As a majorette, Marie entertained the crowds with her baton twirling, while her boyfriend was the team's quarterback. By the end of her junior year, her high school performance in both academics and extracurricular activities opened the possibility of attending any number of top-rated colleges and universities.

Then came the summer of 1958 and the life-altering encounter that would always be a part of her. After her junior year in high school, she joined many of her high school classmates at the Jersey Shore, where older high school students came in droves during the summer months. A young female high school teacher chaperoned Marie and nine other girls while they stayed in a cottage there. The week began with a whirl-wind of social activity as different groups of friends came to their cottage and traveled in packs to the beach. Marie enjoyed the company of this group, all of whom she knew from school.

However, in the middle of the week, an older teen stopped by. He lived down the street from her and was the older brother of one of her girlfriends. Although she knew little about him, she believed that she would be safe with him when he invited her to his motel room to drink some beer.

Once she was inside the motel room, he grabbed her, and Marie suddenly realized that she was trapped and about to be victimized. Isolated from her friends, she had no hope of being rescued, no matter how loudly she screamed. With his superior strength, he overcame her resistance.

After he released her back to her group, Marie thought her life was ruined. She felt such shame that she considered drowning herself in the ocean. The next morning, she walked to the nearest church and rang the doorbell to seek help. The minister came to the door, and Marie explained that she was deeply troubled and needed to talk. When she explained what had happened, the clergyman was decidedly unsympathetic and blamed her for putting herself in that situation. On her walk back to the cottage, Marie again considered taking her own life.

She eventually told a group of her girlfriends what had happened. When her boyfriend arrived later in the day, she told him the entire story. Although he remained silent, his anger was palpable. She sensed that he and some of his football friends would corner her assailant and take revenge. Because they never spoke about this again, she never knew what action, if any, he took.

When she returned home, she decided not to tell her parents or report the rape to the police. No one talked about sexual assaults. As far as she knew, rape didn't happen to people like her, and she felt deeply ashamed and responsible. She would try to bury the memory.

Over the next months and years, she eventually realized that she was not to blame. Her humiliation turned into anger. She had trusted a neighbor who had betrayed her. He had sought her out, isolated her, and overpowered her. She had not invited or encouraged his behavior. The encounter had been about his own sexual gratification, viciously exercised. What he had done was a crime, plain and simple, and it was *not* her fault.

However, she did not want the anger to consume her and fought to move on. Although she tried to keep the memory locked away, it had its own life and escaped when it could. The trigger could be anything—an older man staring at her longer than normal, a teenager who resembled her assailant, or a man walking behind her when she was alone. It was always there, under the surface, ready to pounce. And when it did, she relived the horror and the outrage. She would never forget that the world could become a very ugly place—suddenly and without warning. If she was ever threatened again, she would be ready. But for now, she would try to live life on her own terms.

To the world, she seemed like the same Marie. She did all the things that high school seniors did. She continued to date her longtime boy-friend, the school's quarterback, a quiet and reserved young man with whom she had a close and confiding friendship. With her other friends, she stayed active and involved. In academics, she continued to study hard and excelled. She twirled her baton, not only at football games, but at nursing homes as part of a group of high schoolers who entertained the residents.

In the fall, Marie began her freshman year at Duke University. When she chose Duke, she knew that she would be attending a South-ern school, but she did not comprehend the cultural difference be-tween the North and the South. When Marie saw her first "whites only" drinking fountain, she suddenly realized that she was in the world of Jim Crow and strict segregation. There were no black students at Duke, and although women were admitted, they were outnumbered by their male counterparts four to one. The strict Duke dress code forbade women from wearing slacks to class.

Taking a diverse selection of courses, Marie gravitated toward art history until her ever-practical father told her that she needed to focus on a more traditional major. Prodded in the right direction, Marie be-came a psychology major.

Although Duke had sororities, it did not have sorority houses. Many of the same women lived together in one dormitory for their entire college stay, leading to close female friendships that often lasted a life-time.

It was at Duke that Marie met her future husband, Chuck Grossman. They were both in the same year, but because Chuck was an
electrical engineering student, they had no classes together. Chuck was
first drawn to Marie when he spotted her photograph in a campus
magazine after she had been named a campus "duchess." He was captivated by her pretty face and bided his time, waiting for the opportunity
to ask her out when she was between boyfriends.

Toward the end of their junior year, Marie was "free" again, and
Chuck mustered his courage to ask her for a date. She knew next to
nothing about him—only that he and one of her former boyfriends
were friends and wrestled for the Duke team. On a lark, Marie decided
to go out with him, and to her surprise, they clicked from the start. The
relationship grew more and more serious, and they married soon after
graduation.

Chuck and Marie moved to San Diego, where Chuck worked for
General Dynamics and took some night business courses while Marie
took additional college courses in order to teach school. She did her
student teaching in Southern California and became a certified elementary school teacher. Chuck found his work among two thousand engi-
neers unsatisfying and decided a career switch was in order. He applied
to Harvard Business School and was accepted into its MBA program.

For the next two years, Chuck and Marie lived in the Boston area,
and Marie taught third grade in Malden, Massachusetts. She also tu-
tored at-risk students at the Phillips Work House in south Boston's
Roxbury neighborhood. When Martin Luther King Jr. came to Boston
to protest the city's segregated schools, Marie joined the march.

After Chuck earned his degree, they moved to the Cleveland area,
where Chuck worked in the family business, a company that made fire-
retardant clothing, while Marie found another teaching position. Although she was offered a job in a suburban school system, Marie opted
to teach third grade in Tremont, one of Cleveland's inner-city neighborhoods. Although she loved the children, she found the bureaucracy of
the Cleveland school system stultifying. She had students who could not
read at a third-grade level, yet she was not allowed to select reading
books geared to their abilities. Frustrated, Marie rewrote the books, to
tailor them not only to her students' reading level but to their life
experiences.

Hoping to effect change, she persisted until she received an appointment with the Cleveland superintendent of schools. She explained that the school's rigid reading program caused many students to fall farther behind. Although the superintendent listened attentively, he ultimately did nothing.

Disenchanted by the school system's bureaucracy, Marie concluded that, as a teacher, she would not be able to make a significant impact on the problems facing her students and families. Perhaps a law school education would give her the necessary tools to be an agent for change. Shortly thereafter, she took the LSAT and applied to Case Western Reserve School of Law.

In the fall of 1968, Marie was one of six female students enrolled in Case's first-year law class, part of the first wave of women to seek careers in law. In the following years, law schools would accept more and more women, but in 1968, the women students were often singled out for "special" treatment. Marie's contract law professor told his male students that they didn't need to be prepared for Saturday sessions because he would only be calling on women on those days. Her female counterparts were all bright and conscientious and had no difficulty with this treatment or any other aspect of law school.

Despite becoming pregnant during the first month of law school, Marie thrived during that first year. After final examinations were graded, Marie was ranked second in her class, a position she never relinquished during her three years at Case.

Although motherhood and infant care were added to her daily schedule, she maintained a full-time status throughout her second and third years. In fall 1969, the beginning of her second year, the school's career placement director encouraged her to apply for summer clerkships at Cleveland's three most prestigious law firms. In 1970, she was a summer associate at Cleveland's largest law firm, Jones, Day, Reavis & Pogue. She was treated with respect and enjoyed the projects that various attorneys assigned to her. If the firm tendered her a full-time position when she graduated, she would accept it.

Marie became pregnant for a second time in September of 1970, just as she began her third year in the program. When her class graduated nine months later, she was confined to a hospital room at University Hospitals after giving birth to her and Chuck's second son. From her open hospital room window, she could hear some of the amplified words coming from the nearby graduation ceremony as they drifted over the campus. Jones Day had offered her a position as a first-year associate, and she would start there in a few months.

For the first time, Jones Day permitted its women associates to participate in the partnership track, instead of toiling in subordinate research and support roles. For her first four years at the firm, Marie worked part-time, approximately five and a half hours a day, and increased that to a full-time schedule by 1976. During these years, she worked on corporate matters with some of the firm's top partners. Through these assignments, she was involved in drafting the original incorporation documents for the Playhouse Square Foundation, the nonprofit corporation that saved Cleveland's iconic theaters from the wrecking ball. She also assisted in the legal work that preceded construction of the Richfield Coliseum, the home of the Cleveland Cavaliers basketball team.

Although Marie took pride in turning out quality work, she was not interested in the long work hours that were necessary to become a partner. With two small boys at home, she was ready for the next new adventure, one that would ensure that she could balance her work life with her family. In October of 1978, she accepted a position in the legal department of the Cleveland Trust Company (soon to be renamed AmeriTrust), Cleveland's largest bank.

When Marie came to AmeriTrust, she exuded the confidence of someone who had performed well at a prestigious law firm. In an environment where most of the bank's lawyers were cautious, Marie's advice was usually bold and practical. When asked about the legality of a proposed bank service, she routinely interpreted the law as allowing it. Her mantra was: If the law does not specifically prohibit the activity, then it is permitted. She was a stickler for understanding every provision of a statute and would evaluate it through her own detailed reading, never simply relying on another's interpretation.

Dressed in her custom-made suits, she cut a distinctive figure in the usually staid office of counsel. Her tailored jackets, skirts, and dress shirts projected both power and femininity.

She was always eager to tackle new projects that she hoped would challenge her. When human resources needed an attorney to draft a policy manual, Marie took on that task. Later, when the bank acquired Republic Steel's health claims administration company, Marie was asked to oversee that operation, becoming its de facto CEO. After she'd been running the company for three years, the challenge was gone. Marie needed something new to fuel her interests.

In July of 1987, she resigned from AmeriTrust and began working for Preferred Healthcare. She was charged with developing a network of mental health providers in the greater Cleveland area for the company. It was this job that placed her in the Burger King parking lot on December 11, 1987, and ultimately led to her life's greatest challenge.

3

THE SHOT

With the gun at her temple, it was time to act. Marie took a deep breath as she pressed her right foot down on the accelerator. Immediately, she heard an explosion that rocked her body violently to the right. She knew instantly that she had been shot in the head. Where, she didn't know. Her hands were still clutching the steering wheel, while her right foot slid off the accelerator. Looking down, she saw that her coat was drenched in blood.

I'm still alive, she thought. *I can still think. How is that possible?* She looked to her left and out the open car window. As far as she could tell, the man with the gun was gone. Her car was no longer by the menu board. As if on its own, it had drifted forward, closer to the building.

Looking through the windshield, she could see the Cleveland Clinic's main office tower several blocks away as it loomed over the nearby apartment buildings. *I'm going to bleed to death if I don't get help*, she thought. *I have to take control.* She gently placed her right foot on the accelerator again, drove the car forward, and pulled it even with the restaurant's side door.

Her heart was beating rapidly, pulsing in her eardrums. *I'm alive. I have to remain conscious. I can't pass out*, she told herself. *Get to the Clinic now.* As she unfastened her seat belt, she realized that her lower jaw was hanging over her chest, no longer attached to its upper counterpart. Unable to move her jaw, she realized that she could not talk.

Leaving the motor running, she opened the car door and placed her left hand under her jaw to keep it closed. With her first few steps, she reached the concrete sidewalk. Her high heels clattered over its surface until one heel snagged on a crack and she almost fell. Regaining her balance, she lunged toward the door, opened it, and staggered into the restaurant.

She made her way to the counter, leaving a trail of blood along the way. Except for a few teenaged employees, the restaurant was empty. Seeing her, the young workers froze in their tracks, unsure how to respond. From the counter, she grabbed a pencil and a preprinted pad where employees recorded customer orders. She tore out a page, turned it onto its blank side, and wrote, "Take me to the Cleveland Clinic emergency room."

She handed the paper to a young black man, probably seventeen or eighteen years old. Looking bewildered, he answered, "I'll call 911."

Marie shook her head and grabbed the man by the sleeve. When they got near the door, she pointed to her car.

Glancing over his shoulder, he gave a confused look to a fellow employee, shrugged his shoulders, and followed Marie out of the restaurant. She pointed to the blue Mustang, but he knew it was hers because the motor was still running. He was prepared to open the passenger door for her, but she scurried past him to the passenger side, opened the door herself, and quickly slid in. With an easy tug, he opened his door and was relieved to see that his seat was not puddled with blood. Placing one hand on the steering wheel and the other on the center gear shift, he stole a quick glance at the wild, bloody woman who sat next to him.

He would try not to look at her again. His job was to focus on the traffic and deliver her to the Clinic safely and quickly. What if she bled to death before he got her to the hospital? That didn't seem likely. Although he did not look at her directly, he could see from his peripheral vision that she pointed whenever he was supposed to make a turn. When the car arrived at the main entrance, he watched as she opened the door, swung her legs out, and leaned forward. For a moment, she teetered on her seat's edge and he thought she might fall backward. She lurched forward a second time, managed to stand, and walked cautiously toward the entrance. Through the open passenger door, he watched as she disappeared into the building. He exhaled deeply, closed his eyes, and waited for his heart to stop pounding. He'd done what she'd asked. After a minute, he got out of the car, left the keys with someone at the admissions desk, and walked back to the restaurant.

Once inside the hospital, Marie followed the signs to the emergency room. Although the Cleveland Clinic had an emergency room, it did not have a well-marked exterior entrance. First responders routinely transported gunshot victims like Marie to MetroHealth Medical Center, a tertiary trauma center, or University Hospitals. However, when Marie was placed on a gurney in the Clinic's emergency room, she felt a great sense of relief. *They won't let me die*, she thought. *I'm going to be all right.*

Because she'd dropped her wallet and purse for her assailants, Marie did not have her health insurance card or any identification with her. Fueled by adrenaline, she continued to think quickly and improvise. She took a pen from one of the hospital employees and wrote with it in the air, signaling that she needed paper. Once paper was provided, she wrote her name, her husband's name, and his phone number. She was about to hand the sheet back to the nurse when she realized that she also had to get a message to her son Joe at Hawken School and let him know that she was in the hospital. The nurse took the paper and promised to make the phone calls.

Marie was surprised that her initial care was so minimal. Once wheeled into a treatment cubicle, she'd expected a flurry of activity like she'd seen on television shows. Instead, a nurse fixed a blood pressure cuff around her left arm, while another placed a pillow behind her head.

"On a scale of one to ten with ten being the most intense pain imaginable, how would you rate your pain?" the nurse asked.

The question momentarily confused Marie. She'd been shot in the head and blood had been everywhere, but she was not experiencing excruciating pain. How could that be? Her ears were ringing and she could feel pressure in her jaw, but she did not have screaming pain. She raised her right hand from the bed and held up three fingers.

"Is that all?" the nurse asked.

Marie nodded.

"It's the adrenaline rush," the nurse explained. "It will dull your pain for a while. I'll be back to check on you in a few minutes."

For the next ten minutes, Marie waited alone in the cubicle, and then her husband, Chuck, arrived. The hospital had contacted him as

Marie had directed, but it hadn't disclosed that she'd been shot in the face. He only knew that she'd been injured and her life was not in danger. As he hurried to the hospital from the office Christmas party, he'd guessed that she'd been involved in an auto accident.

He was completely unprepared for what awaited him behind the cubicle's curtain. Upon entering, he immediately fixed his eyes on her chest, where her lower jaw rested in a bloody mess. Shocked by the sight, he quickly ducked out of the room. A minute later, he reentered, a different person, composed and in control of his emotions. He now wore his game face and was prepared to provide support and encouragement.

For Marie, the adrenaline continued to surge through her bloodstream. Armed with a pen, she feverishly scribbled details of the attack onto the bedsheet. Over and over again, she forced herself to visualize the shooter's face. When the time came to identify him, she did not want to fail.

When the Clinic doctors marched in a few minutes later, they arrived in force: a plastic surgeon, an ENT specialist, and their cadre of residents. One doctor gently held her jaw in his left hand while he moved her head from side to side with his right. Several more men in white coats, probably residents, manipulated her head in the same way. The first doctor took over again and carefully opened her mouth, using a penlight to assess the damage within. She listened as they whispered among themselves. A bullet had entered through the left side of her jaw and exited on the right, taking with it jawbone, nerves, muscle, and teeth.

The head of the team introduced himself as James Zins, a plastic surgeon. Putting his face close to Marie's, he told her about their findings and plan of action.

"Marie, this is what we are going to do tonight. Your jaw is broken on each side where a bullet entered and exited. We are going to clean out the wound so that it does not get infected. We will realign your jaw and then wire it into place. You won't be able to open it at all. You have lost a lot of bone, but we'll deal with that later, after the swelling has subsided. Do you understand what I am telling you?"

Marie nodded. She could see that this doctor spoke not only with words but with his eyes—eyes that seemed to radiate empathy.

"There are a couple of things that we're going to do because your jaw will be wired completely shut and you won't be able to breathe through your mouth. Because of that, we'll perform a tracheostomy so that you'll be able to breathe through a tube in your neck if you get congestion in your nose or sinuses. Are you with me?"

Marie nodded again.

"You won't be able to eat any food through your mouth, not even liquids right now, because you won't be able to open your mouth at all. We'll insert a nasoenteric feeding tube down one of your nostrils. It'll snake down through your throat and finally into your stomach. Until we can open up your mouth again, you'll get nourishment through this tube."

He then patted her on the shoulder. "I know this sounds like a lot, but if things go well, we'll be able to pull the tubes in a few weeks." He gave her a reassuring smile and walked out of the cubicle to wash for the surgery.

A few minutes later, an orderly came to wheel her to the operating room. Chuck kissed the top of Marie's head and pressed her right hand.

Around 10:30 p.m., Marie slowly regained consciousness in the recovery room. As the grogginess lifted, she remembered what Dr. Zins had said and realized that her jaw was locked with wires. A thin metal bar rimmed the top of her upper teeth at the gumline, while another bar did the same thing at the bottom of her lower teeth. To prevent any jaw movement, tiny rubber bands were moored on the bars from top to bottom, making it impossible to open her mouth. Although she could not see it, she felt something extending from the outside of her neck and into her throat. Her first impulse was to tear the thing out, but then she realized that this was the tracheostomy tube. Another tube dangled in front of her face, probably oxygen, and seemed to feed into the thing on her neck. She heard a sucking sound coming from the device and willed herself to breathe through it.

Later that evening, a man about her age came into the room. He was of medium build and wore a rumpled brown sport coat. He approached her bed gingerly, as if she were a sleeping baby. It was then that Marie noticed that Chuck was also in the room, and he quickly joined the man at her bedside. The man identified himself as Joseph Nowak, a Cleveland police detective. In a voice no louder than a whisper, he asked, "How are you doing?"

Marie opened her eyes wide, as if to say, "I feel awful. Leave me alone."

Although the detective's eyes met hers, he did not read her thoughts and retreat, but instead plowed on. Despite the lingering effects of the anesthesia, Marie could sense that the detective was excited about something. "I'm here to give you some good news," Nowak began. "We've caught the two guys that did this to you."

Momentarily forgetting about the wires in her jaw, Marie tried to open her mouth to ask some questions. Her jaw muscles clenched for a moment before relaxing in defeat. She grunted instead but apparently not loud enough for anyone to hear.

"Really? That's incredible," Chuck said. "Are you sure you have the right ones?"

"Yes. This should be an open-and-shut case. We have two eyewitnesses to the robbery. They gave us the license plate number of the car they came in."

"There were witnesses?" Chuck asked.

"Well, you see, there is this apartment building that overlooks the back parking lot of this Burger King. It's really a halfway house for women who've recently been released from jail or prison. These women don't have much to do but look out the windows and see what's going on outside. These two women saw these guys in the Burger King parking lot waiting in a car and walking around in the lot for over an hour. They watched them as they got out of the car and approached your wife's car at the drive-thru. They saw one of them point a gun inside the car, and they heard the gun go off. They gave us the license plate number of that car. At first the two men ran from the scene and left the car, and then one of them came back ten minutes later and drove the car away."

"That's unbelievable," Chuck said. Whenever his factory had been vandalized, he'd been lucky to get the police to visit the scene, let alone try to solve the crime. He'd fully expected that Marie's attackers would never be caught.

"Well, there's more. We ran a trace on the plates, and they belong to a Richard Thompson, who lives nearby. We were headed toward his house when his car came toward us on the opposite side of the street. We made a U-turn, got behind it, and put the flashers on. They stopped and parked in a church parking lot. We told them to get out and we cuffed them—oh yeah, we also read them their rights, you know. When we went back to Thompson's car, we shined a flashlight inside it and saw a purse and credit cards sprawled on the front floor. Guess whose name was on the cards." Nowak looked at Chuck expectantly.

"Marie's?" Chuck asked.

"Right. The cards were in your wife's name. We also found a gun in the glove compartment with one shot recently fired. We tested the tall, skinny one for gunshot residue on his right hand, and we're waiting for the results. Neither guy is talking right now. They want lawyers."

"Will Marie have to testify at a trial?" Chuck asked. If she could have talked, Marie would have asked the same question.

"Way too early to know whether this case will go to trial. If we put together a strong case, they'll plead. That's my guess. Tomorrow I'll come back with some photographs, and we'll see if Marie can identify the shooter."

"To be honest, I wasn't very optimistic that this crime would ever be solved. Thank you, Detective," Chuck said.

"I'll be back tomorrow." Looking at Marie and touching her left hand, the detective said, "Is that okay?"

Marie nodded.

Lost in the shuffle, Joe Grossman stood off to the side of the recovery area. After he'd finished his wrestling match, Hawken's headmaster had told him that his mother was hospitalized at the Cleveland Clinic and that one of his teammates' parents would drop him off there. Once at the hospital, he'd found his father, who'd explained what had happened. As that information sank in, Joe realized that his mother would never have been at the Burger King had she not been rushing to get to his match. With that recognition came guilt. He couldn't explain why, but he felt responsible for what had happened.

The detective gave Chuck his card and told him to call if he had any questions. After he left, Chuck and Joe sat down and stared at Marie. Underneath the bandages, her face was swollen and misshapen. To them, she looked exhausted, but she was not. The detective's news had reenergized her mind, though not her body.

Joe yawned, and Chuck concluded that everyone needed sleep. Marie was not in any danger and was in good hands at the hospital. Father and son kissed Marie gently on the top of her head and left.

After they had gone, a nurse dimmed the lights in the room. Before closing her eyes, Marie checked the wall clock. It was 11:45. Try as she might, sleep was impossible. Her thoughts jumped from one topic to the next: the shooter's face, the pain in her jaw, the elation of being alive, the decision to hit the accelerator, the drive to the emergency room, the likelihood of permanent facial disfigurement, and the eventual confrontation with her assailants in the courtroom. She opened her eyes. It felt as if an hour had passed. She looked at the clock again. It was 11:49.

4

LONG DAYS AND LONGER NIGHTS

The nausea engulfed her around 1 a.m. When she threw up a few minutes later, the vomit was trapped, striking her locked teeth like a wave against a breakwall. She momentarily panicked, fearful that the burning liquid would block her tracheostomy and cause her to suffocate. Although swallowing the vomitus was painful, she forced herself to do just that. She willed herself to stay calm. She normally would have turned to deep calming breaths, but how could she now? Her mouth was wired shut, her left nostril was clogged with a tube, and she still lacked confidence when breathing through her tracheostomy.

She felt like she was being kept alive by a maze of tubes and machines. For a woman who had always been in control, this sudden dependence was frightening.

She tried to fight the anxiety, but she worried about a tube disconnecting or becoming clogged. Where were the nurses who were supposed to inspect this patchwork of tubes and review the readings on these machines? It felt like she had been alone for hours, but she knew that couldn't be right. Lacking the strength to shift her body in the bed, she couldn't relieve the burning pain in her neck and back. She reached for her notepad, intending to ask a nurse to reposition her. She lost her grip on the pad and watched it tumble to the floor, like a bird shot from a tree. Nothing was easy.

Her thoughts returned to the detective. What if she couldn't identify her assailant from the photographs he'd bring? Would her shooter go free? Would he come after her? She replayed the events leading up to the gunshot; the shooter's thin face was still seared in her memory. No question—she would be able to make the identification.

Replaying that memory came with a cost. She had seen the face of evil and had felt helpless and terrified in its presence. That thought caused her body to tense and her pulse to quicken. However, she had not been a victim. That was not how the story had ended. Refusing to remain passive, she'd taken a huge risk—a gamble that had saved her life. She had fenced with death and somehow survived. It was a reason to celebrate.

But then she saw his face again and terror returned. Throughout the night, she would ride this emotional roller coaster as fear and elation battled for supremacy.

❄ ❄ ❄

When Detective Nowak walked into her room the next morning, Marie recognized him immediately and lifted her hand to greet him. Chuck rose from his chair and shook the detective's hand. Not bothering to take off his trench coat, Nowak opened his briefcase on the now-vacant chair and brought out a packet of photographs. Before showing them to Marie, he looked at each one and then changed the order.

Standing by her bedside, he asked, "Do you remember me?"

Marie nodded.

"I thought so. I've got some photographs for you to look at. Do you feel like doing that?"

Marie nodded again, this time more vigorously.

"I'd like to put the photos on your blanket and let you have a look. If any of them look like your shooter, you point to it."

Marie nodded, while Chuck took a spot on the other side of the bed, opposite Nowak.

The detective placed six black-and-white photographs in front of her. All were head shots of young African American males, perhaps in their twenties. Only one face was long and thin. Marie placed her right hand over that photograph and then jabbed the air above it with her right index finger, as if adding multiple exclamation points to the end of a sentence.

Detective Nowak smiled. "Is that the man who shot you?"

Marie nodded, her eyes animated.

"You just identified Richard Thompson, a black male, age nineteen. He's the guy we arrested last night. As I told you last night, the women in the halfway house gave us the license plate number of the shooter's car and that car was registered to him. He's got gunshot residue on his right hand. He's the guy."

Detective Nowak looked at Marie for a few moments, letting his words sink in before he spoke again. "Okay. Are you absolutely sure this is the guy who shot you?"

Marie blinked and briefly looked away from the detective. The identification had been easy, almost too easy. If she had been shown photographs of two young black men with long, thin faces, would she have been able to point out her shooter? She dismissed the thought.

She met Nowak's eyes and nodded slowly.

"Did you ever see the other guy?"

Marie shook her head.

"Well, then, no need to put another lineup of photographs in front of you."

Marie shrugged her shoulders.

"If you have questions, your husband can call us."

Marie raised her eyebrows, expressing displeasure.

"Of course, you can call us too, once you can talk again," Nowak said, his eyes involuntarily focusing on Marie's trachea tube.

The detective grabbed the photographs and swept them off her blanket and into his hand like playing cards. He placed them in the open manila folder and closed his briefcase.

"I hope you keep improving and are back home soon." He paused as he weighed his next words and then plunged on. "I know this probably sounds horrible, but you are a pretty lucky lady, you know?"

Marie nodded, and Nowak made his exit.

* * *

A few hours later, Marie's friends Peggy and Gary Kuechle found their way into her tiny room in the ICU. Gary had attended high school with Chuck in nearby Rocky River. Although the two had not been particularly close then, they had reconnected when Chuck had returned to Cleveland after completing his MBA. Soon Gary and his girlfriend—

now wife—Peggy began double dating with Chuck and Marie. They'd remained close friends ever since.

It was Peggy who had spotted a two-paragraph article in the *Cleveland Plain Dealer* that morning about an attempted robbery and had been astonished to learn that Marie had been shot. Peggy and Gary had planned to visit Peg's parents on the East Side that day and decided to stop by the Cleveland Clinic on their way. Although the Clinic posted signs restricting ICU visits to family only, Gary and Peggy had ignored them.

When they entered the room, Marie was lying on the hospital bed with her head only slightly raised. They were surprised to find Marie's face swollen and bandaged and a trachea tube extending from her neck. She looked exhausted, but upon recognizing them, she nodded her head in greeting and her eyes shone. Marie grabbed her notepad and wrote, "Glad to see you!"

For the next five minutes, Marie communicated with head nods and short notes. In this way, she told them that she felt fortunate to be alive and that she was improving. During this exchange, Peggy studied her friend's face and could see blood still matted in her hair. She found a washcloth, wetted it, and began cleaning Marie's scalp and hair. Gary discovered some body lotion near the sink and began massaging Marie's feet. Peggy then combed Marie's hair, an act that boosted Marie's morale. When the Kuechles prepared to leave, Marie grabbed each of their hands and held them for a long time, showing them how much she appreciated their kindness.

☆ ☆ ☆

"Marie, I can't believe this happened to you," said her colleague and friend Leslee Miraldi. "I came just as soon as Chuck called me."

Three days after being shot, Marie was now in a regular hospital room, where she was sitting upright in bed with her notepad at her right side. Leslee had expected to find her friend extremely weak and fragile, perhaps close to death, but instead found her very much alive and animated as she wrote on her notepad.

"Feeling stronger every day," Marie wrote. "I have been walking the halls to exercise."

The two had first met nine years earlier, in the fall of 1978. Both had taken jobs at AmeriTrust's office of counsel. Leslee had arrived first, straight out of law school and learning how to actually practice law, something a law school's academic curriculum failed to address. A few months later, the polished Marie had joined the legal team after six years at Cleveland's most prestigious law firm, Jones Day. Marie had quickly taken the young lawyer under her wing, not only guiding her in the law but mentoring her about life in general. She had impressed upon her younger colleague the benefits of a healthy diet and daily exercising, taking her to her favorite restaurants and introducing her to aerobic programs at the Thirteenth Street Racquet Club. Later, when Leslee had children, Marie counseled her on finding balance between work and family.

Several months earlier, Marie had told Chuck that if anything ever happened to her, he was to call Leslee, seeing in her protégée a younger version of herself—a practical problem solver. At 9 a.m. this morning, Chuck had called her and described what had happened to his wife. Leslee dispatched her mother-in-law to babysit her infant and preschooler and was at Marie's side two hours after receiving the call.

Upon seeing Leslee, Marie grabbed her notepad and began writing quickly and energetically. She let her friend know that she planned to be back to her former self as soon as possible. Just before the shooting, she'd been in the best physical shape of her life. Leslee recalled that Marie had implemented rigorous fitness and health regimes after sessions at Canyon Ranch, a health resort. Marie credited those programs with her current resilience. "I want to regain what I've lost," Marie wrote.

As Marie was writing another note, a physician walked into the room. Leslee looked at Marie and said, "Do you want me to ask questions for you?"

Marie nodded emphatically and then rapidly rolled her hands over one another in a circular motion, like a football referee signaling illegal procedure. She wanted Leslee to ask the questions that her wired jaw would not permit her to ask.

Over the next ten minutes, Leslee grilled the doctor about Marie's situation. How much longer would she be in the hospital? What damage had occurred? How long would she have the trach? When would the wires be removed from her jaw? When would she be able to eat through her mouth and not through the nasogastric tube? Was there any permanent damage? Were further surgeries likely? Although the doctor hedged with his answers, he said that Marie would probably be released in several days. Everything looked good at this point. She had lost considerable bone, but he hoped that her body would produce new bone to replace what had been destroyed. The trach and NG tubes could possibly be removed in another week.

"I don't know if you'll need more surgeries, and I can't tell you if you'll have any limitations after you've completed all the treatment. We'll know much more in the coming weeks as the bone fills in. This much is certain—you are very fortunate that the bullet missed your tongue. If it had not, who knows if you'd ever be able to talk normally again? You're very lucky."

After the doctor left, Leslee said, "He seems very optimistic."

The two women sat in silence for a few moments. Marie's face took on a grave expression. "They arrested the guys who did this," she wrote.

"That's what Chuck told me," Leslee responded.

"I'm very scared to face them, but I will go to all of their court hearings," Marie wrote.

"Are you sure you want to do this before you're feeling better?"

Marie nodded and then placed the notepad and pen onto her bed.

Leslee could see that Marie looked very tired and was signaling that it was time for her to leave.

"I think you need some rest. I'll go now."

Marie nodded again and closed her eyes.

❀ ❀ ❀

Chuck Grossman and his son Joe stood in their living room, watching as Marie slept on a recliner. They'd brought her home yesterday, six days after she'd been shot. There she lay: her face swollen and bruised, her chest rising and falling as she took in air from her trach, and her nose red from the tube that descended into her stomach. Father and son looked at each other, their glances betraying anxiety and pity. For Joe, he could hardly believe that this sleeping person was his mother. Her face had become someone else's, not his pretty mom's. For Chuck, he worried whether he'd be able to coordinate all of her home care.

He reassured himself that a nurse would be arriving at 10 a.m. to change the dressing, feed his wife through her tube, and attend to any other needs. He had done his part, gathering the supplies and arranging the living room for her convalescence. When she awakened at 9:30, he helped her walk to the bathroom and waited outside, ready to assist if she beckoned him. A few minutes later they returned to the living room, and Chuck gave her the morning paper to read while they waited for the nurse. At 10:30, Chuck called the home nursing agency to find out why the nurse hadn't arrived. Chuck could hear the scheduler fumbling with papers before she cleared her throat.

"I guess there has been a little mix-up. There's no nurse coming this morning, but one is scheduled for later in the afternoon."

"Can't you get somebody here before then? My wife needs to eat."

"We're a little shorthanded right now, but someone will be there around 2 p.m.," she said, her voice bright and cheerful, in sharp contrast to the bad news she was delivering. She didn't apologize for the mistake.

Chuck looked at the floor, where nutrition packets were stacked neatly in the open box next to the recliner. In the hospital, he'd watched the nurses open a thick plastic bag, attach it to the tube, and gently squeeze the contents down the tube.

"I guess I can do it," Chuck said.

Marie gave him a shrug that seemed to say, "What do we have to lose?"

And he was able to do it, just as he was able to change her dressing. After she'd been fed, he accompanied his wife when she asked to walk up and down the driveway. Back in the house, she wrote that her chin burned from its contact with the cold air but she was very glad that they'd done it. As unnerving as all of this was, they both felt a sense of accomplishment.

Marie wrote, "Can you believe I was shot in the head and can do all of this?" Chuck thought he saw a hint of a smile surfacing from his wife's swollen and wired mouth. But that was impossible, wasn't it? Then it struck him. *It's her eyes—she's smiling with her eyes.*

* * *

Once word got out that Marie was home, a steady stream of friends stopped by, none staying much longer than fifteen minutes. They dropped off casseroles, cakes, and fruit for Chuck and Joe. Others sent flowers—so much so that they joked that the living room smelled like a funeral parlor. The outpouring of love from family and friends buoyed her spirits.

A few days later, her son Chas came home from college on his Christmas break. After his mother had been shot, Chas had been distraught and wanted to come home immediately to see her. Chuck convinced him to stay at school until he had completed his exams. He was home now and could finally see the devastating injuries for himself and help her get through these difficult days.

Her parents arrived from New Jersey a few days before Christmas. Knowing how close she had come to death, Marie celebrated their presence, overlooking the noise and confusion associated with a full house.

Her father, a man she had always thought of as calm and controlled, showed another side during this visit. She overheard him tell Chuck that he wanted to get a gun and take justice into his own hands. Joe Choborda, the man who had grown up on the tough streets of Newark, was outraged by what had happened to his daughter. He was not cowed by the thought of confronting the punks who were responsible. Chuck told him that Marie's assailants were in jail and would likely spend years in prison. Later, Marie exacted a promise from him that he would not do anything rash.

Three days before Christmas, she returned to the Cleveland Clinic. Dr. Zins removed the NG tube, while Dr. Benjamin Wood pulled the trachea hardware, explaining that the tracheostomy site would eventually close spontaneously. Her surgical sites showed no signs of infection. The doctors and their assistants told her that all was progressing perfectly. Despite the fact that her jaw was still wired shut, she would now be able to sip liquids through her mouth.

She couldn't believe her good fortune. In a few weeks, the bands holding her jaw rigidly in place would be removed. Was it really possible that in a few months she'd be completely healed and everything would return to normal? No, she mustn't get ahead of herself. Dr. Zins had been noncommittal when she'd asked about the possibility of future surgeries. Her jaw still throbbed with pain, interrupting her sleep and leaving her constantly fatigued. Trapped beneath the wires and bands, her tongue felt sluggish and numb. She knew that the tongue was instrumental in forming sounds for speech. What if she could never speak normally again? The bullet had obliterated jawbone and teeth. Had any nerves been severed in the process too? And why did these feelings of anxiety and vulnerability periodically overwhelm her? Pushing them away was exhausting. How long would that last?

Still, she had been very lucky. She was home and surrounded by the love of family and friends. Her ability to think was unimpaired, and her body and limbs moved freely. She would remain optimistic. That was just who she was.

5

CONFRONTATION

The late afternoon sun was streaming into Marie's home office when the phone on her desk began ringing. Asleep in the adjoining living room, Marie did not hear it, but Chuck did. He tiptoed by his wife and entered the home office, grabbing the phone before it awakened her. Since returning home from the hospital, Marie had rarely been able to sleep for more than an hour or two at a time. The swelling and pain on each side of her face made it hard to rest her head. The arch bars that kept her jaw rigid were attached with little wires that dug into the surrounding tissue, creating constant pain.

Chuck reached the phone by the third ring. "Hello," he said, trying to keep his voice low but just loud enough for the caller to hear him.

The man's voice on the other end was husky, perhaps the result of chain-smoking. He mumbled his name and then told Chuck that he was an assistant prosecutor for the city of Cleveland. He wanted to speak to Marie.

"You know Marie can't talk. She has a trachea tube in her neck, and her mouth is wired shut," Chuck explained, trying not to sound peeved at the attorney's ignorance about his wife's condition.

There was a long silence on the other end.

"You know she was shot in the jaw at close range, don't you?" Chuck finally said.

The man cleared his throat. "Yes, I guess I knew that from the police report."

"She can give a written statement if that's what you're after," Chuck said.

"No, that's not it. We have a preliminary hearing coming up on December twenty-ninth and I wanted Marie to testify," the prosecutor said.

"Well, that's impossible," Chuck replied.

"Will she ever be able to talk again?"

"Yes, but we don't know when. She had a tracheostomy, and the tube was just removed a few days ago. Her jaw is still wired shut," Chuck answered. "She's not sleeping well. She has flashbacks about the shooter pointing the gun at her. Maybe you can get the hearing postponed until Marie is in better shape."

"We can't get the hearing continued. All defendants have a constitutional right to a speedy trial," the attorney said. He was silent for about twenty seconds; Chuck wondered whether the line had gone dead.

"Are you still there?" Chuck asked.

"Oh, sorry, I'm just thinking," the prosecutor responded. "I have an idea, but let me talk it over with another attorney and I'll be back in a minute. Can you hold?"

"Sure," Chuck said, not wanting the prosecutor to call again and awaken his wife.

After about a minute, the attorney came back on the line. "Could she just come into the courtroom and point out the man who shot her? She wouldn't have to say anything."

"She's sleeping right now, but give me your name again and your phone number and I'll call you later today after I talk to her. Is that okay?"

The attorney said yes and provided his contact information.

Placing the phone carefully back into its receiver, Chuck slumped in the desk chair and stared at the broken golden light as it came through the blinds and warmed the carpet. Before the phone call, he'd hovered somewhere between weary and exhausted. The hospital had discharged Marie on December 17, only six days after the surgery—much too soon in Chuck's opinion. To make matters worse, home health aides had sporadically appeared, oblivious to the chaos their absences created.

Until then, Chuck had never appreciated all the things Marie did effortlessly to make his life run smoothly. Besides working a full-time schedule, she'd always handled the family's child care, household chores, and meals, allowing him to concentrate on his business and play golf on Saturdays. Then this inconceivable thing had happened and his life seemed to be one crisis after another. For the first time, his capable wife was dependent upon him. He'd been thrust into changing dressings, cleaning her trachea tube, and feeding her through another tube. And somehow, he'd managed. He could also sense when she was getting frustrated or depressed, and he'd become her cheerleader.

When she awakened from her nap, he told her about the phone call. She grabbed her notepad and wrote, "I want to go to the hearing."

"Are you sure?" Chuck asked.

"I have to go," she wrote back.

"Okay, we'll go then," he answered. "I'll call the prosecutor back and let him know." Chuck walked into the office and dialed the attorney.

While Chuck did this, Marie thought about her decision. From her law school education, she knew something about criminal procedure. At a preliminary hearing, a judge was required to find probable cause that a crime had been committed; otherwise a defendant could be released. Although a grand jury could later gather evidence and decide to indict, Marie wanted no gap in the defendants' incarceration.

However, the thought of confronting her shooter in the courtroom filled her with terror. Maybe she should tell the prosecutor that she was too weakened or traumatized to attend right now. She quickly dismissed the thought. How could she *not* participate? The defendants were dangerous men who needed to remain locked up in jail and off the streets. But there was another, more compelling reason for her resolve. Deep inside, she knew that she had to face the man who had shot her. She would do so calmly and deliberately; she was no coward. She would look Richard Thompson in the eye and identify him as the person who had pointed a gun at her head and fired it. She would show the world and herself that she was not afraid.

* * *

On the morning of December 29, Chuck drove Marie to the Cuyahoga County Justice Center, a twenty-six-story, honeycombed skyscraper that housed the Cleveland Police Department, the Cleveland Municipal Court, and the Cuyahoga County Court of Common Pleas. The building's stark and drab interior gave it a steel coldness that prevailed regardless of the season. Completed just eleven years earlier, the modern building already seemed out-of-date with its overcrowded bank of elevators and long lines of people waiting to pass through security screens.

Marie and Chuck took an elevator to the fourteenth floor, where they waited, as instructed, in the hallway outside of Courtroom 14B. Wearing a long navy-blue overcoat, Marie decided to keep her plaid scarf wrapped around the lower part of her face in order to hide the swelling and distortion. Although the trachea tube had been removed a week earlier, she still had a hole in her neck that had not yet closed over. The NG tube was gone too, allowing her to breathe through her nose once again. However, talking was another matter. Her mouth was still wired shut; it was impossible for her to make any sounds other than unintelligible grunts.

Unable to sleep the night before, Marie should have been exhausted. However, for now, her nervousness was keeping her weariness at bay. She watched people huddled in groups of two and three in the hall. Some talked in whispers while others were loud and angry. She wondered whether anyone from Richard Thompson's family would appear. Shivering, she placed her gloved hands in her overcoat's large pockets.

An elevator door opened, expelling six more people. Scanning the group, Marie was relieved to recognize Detective Nowak, who was talking to a young man in a gray suit, probably her prosecutor. Nowak held a manila folder in his right hand and waved with his left after he spotted her and Chuck. The assistant prosecutor introduced himself as Peter Young. Marie guessed that this slight man, barely five feet nine, was perhaps thirty years old. She hoped he knew what he was doing.

"I talked to your husband last week," Young said. "You'll just need to stand up and point to Richard Thompson when I ask you to identify the man who shot you."

Marie nodded.

"Detective Nowak will do all the heavy lifting today. You won't have to do much at all," Young said. He suddenly looked embarrassed. "But thanks for coming. Your identification is important to our case."

Marie nodded and Chuck looked away, upset that the prosecutor didn't seem to value the sacrifice his wife had made to be there.

The prosecutor continued, "Why don't you go inside and have a seat in the courtroom until the hearing begins? Detective Nowak and I are going to speak in the hallway for a short time. We'll join you in a few minutes."

The judge was not in the courtroom. An attorney sat on the edge of one trial table and swung his feet under it, his paperwork splayed haphazardly behind him. In one corner, an attorney was talking to a client. Marie and Chuck sat on a wooden bench directly behind the court rail. A few minutes later, Detective Nowak and Prosecutor Young entered and sat down at the other trial table.

Young immediately got up and walked over to Chuck and Marie. "We'll get started in just a few minutes. We're waiting for the sheriff's deputies to bring up Richard Thompson."

The attorney who had been swinging his feet stood up and walked over to the prosecutor. The two talked quietly for a few minutes before the courtroom doors opened. Marie pivoted to look behind her and saw Thompson, flanked by two deputies. He was wearing an orange jail jumpsuit, his hands still handcuffed and his long brown arms extending from his sleeves like sticks. He looked down at his feet, never seeing or acknowledging Marie.

"Is that him?" Chuck whispered to his wife.

Marie sat frozen, unable to respond with a simple nod. The man who had shot her sat not more than eight feet in front of her. She wondered if any words would have come out even if she could have spoken. She started to breathe rapidly and could feel her heart pulsing in her ears.

"He's so tall and thin," Chuck said. Even when slumped, Thompson could not hide his six-feet-five-inch frame. "He can't weigh more than a hundred fifty pounds."

As Marie stared at the back of Thompson's head, her pulse and breathing began to slow. Her assailant looked straight ahead, apparently gazing at the bronze state seal that hung on the front wall. Perhaps Thompson had caught a glimpse of her when he'd walked into the courtroom and now was afraid to turn around and look at her. This thought emboldened her.

She took off her winter gloves and placed them beside her on the bench. She rubbed her hands together and noticed that they were warm and dry. She was ready.

The judge sat down and began his preliminary remarks. Marie fidgeted with her gloves, picking them up, squeezing them, smoothing them, and then placing them back on the bench. As the judge talked, she checked her wristwatch several times. Marie's thoughts returned to the ICU room on the night of the shooting. Once again, it seemed like time was refusing to move forward. She took a deep breath and exhaled as loudly as she could through her wired mouth. Didn't the judge realize that she wanted to make her identification?

"Mr. Young, who is your first witness?"

"We will call Detective Joseph Nowak," the prosecutor replied.

The detective rose slowly, sat in the witness chair, and instinctively raised his right hand even before the bailiff began to swear him in. He pulled a report from his manila folder and waited for the prosecutor's first question. After providing background information about his position with the Cleveland police force, he began to outline his investigation of a robbery involving someone named Brittany Kirkpatrick at the Burger King parking lot at 8515 Euclid Avenue.

Marie and Chuck looked at one another in confusion. Didn't the detective know Marie's name?

"The date and time of the robbery at the drive-thru, Detective Nowak?" Young asked.

"October 24, 1987, at approximately 11:40 p.m."

"Please go on," the prosecutor urged.

"Ms. Kirkpatrick stated that two men came running toward her car when she was stopped at the drive-thru menu board. She tried to roll up the driver's-side window, but before she could, one of the men reached the car and put a gun to her head and ordered her to unlock the door. He climbed into the backseat while another man got into the front passenger seat."

Marie listened incredulously as the detective detailed a prior robbery at the same Burger King involving the same men who'd attempted to get into her car. She pulled a pad of paper from her purse, nudged Chuck in the ribs, and wrote, "Did you know about this?"

He shook his head and raised his eyebrows.

"They demanded to see her 'asset card' so that they could withdraw money from her account. When she claimed she didn't have one, they told her to drive.around while they searched her purse. They took money from her purse and told her to stop the car. For a few minutes, they argued about whether to release her. They eventually ordered Ms. Kirkpatrick out of the car and then drove her car away. Ms. Kirkpatrick has identified Christopher Martin as one of the two men from a lineup. She will identify him later this afternoon at Mr. Martin's preliminary hearing. She described the other man as an African American, tall and thin, but could not identify him from a lineup."

While the detective talked, Marie began to remember more about preliminary hearings from her criminal law class at Case Western Reserve. The state's burden of proof was low; the prosecutor simply needed to present enough evidence to justify a reasonable belief that the defendant had committed the crime. She also recalled that hearsay testimony was permitted, thus allowing investigating detectives like Nowak to summarize the testimony of their principal witnesses.

"Any other investigations, Detective Nowak?"

Nowak pulled another packet of papers from his folder and began reading directly from his report. "Yes. On November 14, 1987, at around 10:50 p.m., a Carol Thornton was awaiting service at the drive-thru menu board at a Popeyes restaurant located at 8210 Euclid Avenue when a man with a gun approached her driver's-side window. He told her to move over and pointed a gun at her neck. The man unlocked all of the doors, and a second man got into the rear seat. The first man drove her car out of the parking lot onto Euclid Avenue, while Ms. Thornton sat in the front passenger seat."

Marie looked at Chuck again. *How many women have these men terrorized?* Marie thought.

"One of the men asked her to pull out her wallet from her purse and get her 'asset card.' She told them that she didn't have an 'asset card,' and the two got angry. She suddenly realized that they wanted any bank withdrawal card and told them she had a bank card from Bank One. The men drove around briefly while they discussed which location to make a withdrawal. Ms. Thornton encouraged them to take her to a bank machine at Cedar and Fairmount because she was familiar with the area." Nowak's tone was unemotional, almost deadpan.

I am not alone. Here are two women who experienced almost the same things as I did. I need to talk to them. Marie's fingers quivered, and then she drew both hands into tight fists.

Nowak continued to read in a monotone. "When they arrived at this location, the man in the backseat took the gun and accompanied Ms.

Thornton as she withdrew two hundred fifty dollars, the maximum permitted. He then instructed her to make a second withdrawal of fifty dollars and Thornton did so. They then ordered her back into the car, and the men drove around for a while, debating what to do next. Finally, the men ordered Thornton out of her car and drove away."

Where are Carol Thornton and Brittany Kirkpatrick? Why aren't they at the preliminary hearing?

Detective Nowak stopped reading his report and looked at the prosecutor. "Ms. Thornton identified Christopher Martin as one of the two assailants from a lineup, and she will identify him in open court this afternoon at Mr. Martin's preliminary hearing." Nowak paused and switched his gaze to the judge to clarify his last point. "Mr. Martin was the one who pulled the gun on her and then drove her car. She described the other man—the one in the backseat—as an African American, very tall and thin, somewhere between the ages of eighteen and twenty-five, but she couldn't positively identify Mr. Thompson as the other man."

Now it was clear. Marie was here because she was the only person who could identify Richard Thompson as the "other man" and tie him to this pattern of robbery. She was the linchpin that could convict him of not just one crime but three. Her heart fluttered, and a wave of nervousness passed through her and settled in her stomach.

She listened as Detective Nowak described what had happened to her. He told the judge about his investigation: the witnesses in the halfway house; the license plate number of the robber's car; stopping that car and finding Marie's purse, wallet, and credit cards in it; the gun; the gun residue results; and the fact that Marie had identified Thompson in a photo lineup.

Prosecutor Young interrupted Nowak's testimony. "The State would like to ask Ms. Grossman to be sworn at her seat, to stand, and to identify the man who shot her. As a word of explanation, Ms. Grossman was shot through the jaw, her jaw is wired shut, and she has just recently been released from the hospital. She can't talk."

The judge nodded. "Mr. Thompson, stand up and face Mrs. Grossman."

Thompson looked at his lawyer as if expecting him to object. Instead, his attorney nodded at him, and Thompson slowly got to his feet. His shoulders slumped as he turned to face the gallery. Instead of looking straight ahead, he looked to his left. Marie stood up, her five-feet-three-inch frame dwarfed by the much taller man just several feet away. As Thompson swayed slightly from left to right, she studied his features. This was the face of the man who'd held a gun inches from her temple. She tried not to look scared. She reached down to the bench and grabbed her notepad and pen. She wrote, "This is the man who shot me. I am sure of it."

She nodded to the judge and then handed the note to Prosecutor Young.

The prosecutor read the note in open court. He then asked several more questions of the detective. When it was his turn to cross-examine, Thompson's attorney declined. After brief statements by both attorneys, the judge found probable cause and maintained Thompson's bond at $15,000. The indigent Thompson would stay in jail until the grand jury heard his case and indicted him.

6

SETBACK

Marie thought that she would be able to talk as soon as the tube was removed from her throat, but the tracheostomy had inflamed the tissue near her voice box. She also had an opening in her throat that needed to heal before she could effectively activate the larynx. Despite her inability to talk, she refused to stay home. As the new year began, she drove herself to nearby River Oaks to participate in various aerobics classes. Freed from the tube feedings, Marie experimented with healthy liquid concoctions to sip through her still-wired jaw. After she read the contents of the recommended Ensure drink, she was shocked to learn that it was largely corn syrup and sucrose. As a result, she experimented with her own much healthier substitutes, various blends of fruits and vegetables pureed in a Cuisinart.

One morning in early January, she found that she could speak. Even though she could not open her mouth and her wired jaw allowed very little movement, she could talk. It was similar to speaking through clenched teeth—not what she wanted right now but a vast improvement over the constant scribbling. After more than a month of writing out each and every communication, she marveled at the spontaneity of speech.

When the bands were removed by a Cleveland Clinic nurse two weeks later, she could open her jaw, albeit only a few millimeters. She could hardly contain her delight over this insignificant change. She felt liberated—as if someone had jimmied her jail cell's door just enough to allow her to escape. The nurse gave her some tongue blades to place between her molars to gradually increase the opening in her jaw.

The next morning, Marie awakened with intense pain in her jaw, particularly at the joint where the upper and lower jaws met. She didn't want to overreact, but by noon, the pain reached excruciating levels. She arranged to see Dr. Zins again. When he took panoramic X-rays of her jaw, he quickly saw the problem. The shattered pieces of jawbone had not fused together while Marie's jaw had been immobilized. Instead, the fragments had been resorbed by other tissue, leaving a gap in both the left and right sides of her jaw where the bullet had traveled in and out. Dr. Zins explained that the jaw would not heal without at least one or two more surgeries.

Dr. Zins told her that the next surgery would be a complicated one. He would realign both sides of the jaw and then rigidly fix the left side in place with a metal plate and take bone from her hip to fill the gap on the jaw's right side. He warned that the opening moments of the surgery could be very unpleasant. An anesthesiologist would have to snake a tube down her nose while she was conscious to intubate her for the anesthesia because her mouth and throat needed to remain clear for the jaw surgery. After the surgery, she would be wired shut again for another month. Because he would be harvesting bone from her hip and tackling the nonunion of two jaw fractures, the surgery could last anywhere from six to eight hours.

"I understand why you need to do this surgery, but I don't know why I may still need another surgery after this one," Marie said. She'd anticipated that her recovery would be steady and that she would gradually gain more and more function, but this news meant a step backward. She would be wired shut again, not just another time but perhaps two more.

"This surgery will be long enough as planned. I am hoping that the plate and the bone graft will be all that you'll need. If we need another bone graft on the other side, we'll have to do that later."

Marie looked unconvinced. *Why couldn't he just do both bone grafts at the same time? It can't be that much longer to do two.*

As if reading her mind, Dr. Zins said, "I don't want you to be under general anesthesia any longer than what's absolutely necessary. Let's be optimistic and hope that I won't have to go in again."

"How soon will you do this?"

"They're checking my schedule right now. I think in two weeks, maybe a little sooner."

Marie nodded, her face a picture of resignation.

"For now, we'll put the bands back on. That should reduce the pain that you're experiencing. I'll also prescribe some Valium." He took her hand. "I know you're disappointed, but this was a very destructive bullet that tore through your jaw. You'll get through this. I promise."

Marie liked this doctor. He had a quiet manner and eyes that showed his genuine concern. He had delicately delivered the bad news. She had no choice but to accept it and move forward.

Once home, she told Chuck through her rebanded jaw that she would require one or two more surgeries. Although she put on a brave face, Chuck realized that Marie was depressed and unnerved by this development.

"Let's go to Hilarities tonight," he suggested. Whenever he sensed that Marie's morale needed a boost, he proposed a trip to this Cleveland comedy club located in the Warehouse District, an area close to the Cuyahoga River that was just beginning to transform itself into Cleveland's new entertainment and restaurant venue. The club's large room was conveniently dark, which allowed them to slip into a back table where no one could see Marie's swollen face.

Marie nodded her assent and then lay on the living room couch. This was not what she had foreseen. She'd expected to regain her strength and speech this month and return to work soon thereafter. Now her future was clouded by uncertainty—at least one and maybe two major jaw reconstructions with long, painful recovery periods. What if her jaw was hopelessly mangled with no surgical solution? Even if it were "fixed," would she still have jaw pain and associated headaches for the rest of her life? And then there were the upcoming criminal hearings involving her shooter, Richard Thompson. Would she be able to attend them? Would she be healthy enough to testify at his trial if she had just undergone a surgery? These thoughts made it impossible to nap.

A few days later, the prosecutor's secretary phoned to tell her about Richard Thompson's upcoming pretrial. After the preliminary hearing, Thompson and Martin had been indicted by a Cuyahoga County grand jury. Their cases had been transferred from municipal court to the county court, where they would be prosecuted by one of the Cuyahoga County assistant prosecutors, Robert Christyson. She'd left him a message, requesting that his office call her whenever hearings were scheduled.

"The first pretrial is scheduled for February tenth at 2 p.m. Mr. Christyson said that you wanted to attend. It's not necessary, but you are welcome to observe. Generally, he just talks with the defense attorney in private—you know, in a jury room—and then they report to the judge or staff attorney."

Marie was pleased that this assistant prosecutor was keeping her in the loop. "I'd like to be there, but unfortunately I'm undergoing surgery on February ninth and I'll be in the hospital. When I'm discharged from the hospital, can I call him to find out what's happening on the case?"

"Oh, certainly, you can call him. I'm sorry that you're going to have another surgery. I hope it's not serious?"

"Well, yes. My jawbones are not healing, and they have to do some special things to fix them."

The secretary wished her well and said good-bye.

* * *

On February 9, Marie was wheeled into the operating room at the Cleveland Clinic. She'd forgotten Dr. Zins's disclosure about the intubation through her nose. As the anesthesiologist began pushing the tube through her nose and down her throat, she thought she would gag. *I'm not getting enough air. I'm going to suffocate.* She closed her eyes and tried to remain calm, but how could she? She opened her eyes, only to see two large hands looming over her nose, blocking any view of the operating room. She felt the tube grind its way down the back of her throat. If she could have opened her jaw wide enough to scream, she would have.

One of the doctors said, "More Ativan. Increase the Ativan."

In a few moments, she felt her body relaxing, and then she was out. When she regained consciousness after the eight-hour surgery, she was in the recovery room. As the anesthesia dissipated, pain increased on both sides of her jaw, her throat, and her left hip. Had she hurt this badly after the first surgery? Two months ago, she'd been euphoric that she'd miraculously survived a gunshot to the head. Back then her racing thoughts had kept her awake, but now it was the unrelenting pain.

Today, her jaw, still reeling from the prior trauma, had received further insult. It was no wonder that the jaw pain was unrelenting, but now she also had left-hip and throat pain to contend with.

Four days later, she was home again. She knew that the bands would remain on her jaw for another three weeks, but because she had no trachea tube, she could talk through the wired jaw. Her first phone call was to Assistant Prosecutor Christyson. He told her that both defendants were still in jail, unable to post bond. At an earlier arraignment, both men had been found indigent, and the judge had appointed separate counsel to defend them. At the pretrial, both criminal defense attorneys had wanted copies of the police investigation and any exculpatory evidence—things they were entitled to under the criminal rules of discovery.

"Is there anything exculpatory in the file?" Marie asked as she squeezed the pen in her hand.

"No, there's nothing to suggest that somebody else was involved. It's unfortunate that you didn't get a look at Christopher Martin's face. I'll have to demonstrate that these two guys worked together all the time and had developed a signature MO for robbing people at fast-food restaurants."

"Will that be enough to convict Martin?" Marie asked. Could the accomplice be acquitted and soon be back on the street? Would she ever be safe?

"We'll have a final pretrial on February twenty-fifth and a trial on March first. I'm fairly confident that we'll convict Martin of the two other robberies. The other two women are certain that Martin was one of the two men who robbed them, but your case against him is not strong," the prosecutor replied.

"I never dreamed the case would come to trial this quickly," Marie said.

"I don't think it will, but neither defendant has signed anything to waive a speedy trial, so we have to be ready. I think they'll sign a waiver, but if they don't, that's when their cases will be tried."

"As you can tell, I cannot talk very well. The bands should come off by the end of the month, and I should be able to speak more clearly by then," Marie said, more to reassure herself than to provide further information to the prosecutor.

"Here's the thing," the prosecutor said. Marie noted hesitation in his voice. "I wouldn't normally tell this to a victim, but because you're a lawyer, I'll let you know something. We're having discussions with Richard Thompson's attorney about his client testifying against Chris Martin."

"Really? Why would you do that?" Marie asked. Did this mean that her shooter might get a light sentence? She clenched her wired jaw even tighter.

The prosecutor drew in a breath, and there was an awkward pause before he responded. "Right now, two victims have identified Christopher Martin as one of the two men who abducted and robbed them. You are the only one who ID'd Richard Thompson. The other two women couldn't identify Thompson as one of the men who abducted them. Our cases against him in the other two robberies are weak."

"Go on," Marie responded. She held the cordless phone to her ear and began pacing in her kitchen.

"Don't worry. If we cut—I mean, make a deal with Thompson, he'll have to plead guilty to your crime and we'll be able to lock him up for a long time. If he testifies against his buddy, we'll likely drop the charges against him in the other two robberies."

"Oh," Marie said, not sure if she liked what she was hearing.

"Thompson will spend years in prison. Don't worry about that. Our judge is Carl Character. He's an African American, and he's tough," he said, his voice turning defensive. "If we can get Thompson's help, Christopher Martin will be in there even longer. Martin's got a record; Thompson does not. Thompson seems anxious to plead out and cooperate. Martin denies any involvement in these three robberies. His lawyer says he's got alibi witnesses."

"But still . . . ," Marie said, her voice trailing off.

"Remember, you never saw the other guy, only your shooter. If Martin's attorney can throw doubt on the other victims' identification, Martin might walk—unless we get Thompson's testimony."

"I see," Marie answered. "If he gets a deal, how long will Thompson remain in prison?"

"That's up to the judge, but there are gun specifications with these crimes and there are mandatory prison sentences associated with them. Don't hold me to this, but he could be locked up for a good ten years."

"Uh-huh," she said, wanting to believe Christyson, but she was skeptical. She'd read about overworked prosecutors who cut deals that incensed the victims. Was Christyson one of them? Was this going to happen to her too?

Sensing trouble, the prosecutor tried to calm her. "We've got a chance to put both of these guys away for a long time, not just one."

"Well, this is a lot to digest right now."

This time the prosecutor remained silent while he allowed Marie to think.

"What you're suggesting makes sense," Marie finally said, her voice tenuous. "You'll let me know if there are any new developments."

"I will."

* * *

The next development involved not the criminal case but the need for the third surgery. The sutures were removed two weeks after the second surgery, and once again, after the bands were removed, Marie started jaw exercises with tongue blades and gradually increased her jaw opening one millimeter at a time. She was alarmed when she could not move her jaw from right to left at all. After Dr. Zins took additional X-rays, he told her that the third surgery was indeed needed. She suspected that Dr. Zins had known this all along but had not wanted to give her too much discouraging news earlier.

This time he would harvest bone from her right hip and add it to the missing bone at the left mandibular angle. On the right side, he would place a new metal reconstruction plate.

"Will I be intubated through the nose?" Marie asked.

"Yes, we'll have to do that one more time."

"I don't think I can stand that again," she said, shaking her head to emphasize her concern.

"I know it's tough. I'll ask the anesthesiologist to make you more sedated this time."

"That was a real nightmare," Marie continued. "I know I'm going to worry about this for the next three weeks."

After she returned home, she called the prosecutor to advise him of the upcoming surgery on March 23. He was not in, but his secretary promised to relay the message.

An hour later, the prosecutor called back. "I was meaning to call you. We had another pretrial on February twenty-fifth, and Thompson will plead guilty to charges stemming from your incident. He'll also turn state's evidence against Martin. Both defendants signed waivers for a speedy trial, and Martin's trial, which was set for March first, has been continued until March thirty-first. Will that be a problem for you?"

"Yes, that will be. I probably won't be released from the hospital until the twenty-seventh or so. I don't think I'll be in any condition to come to court. My jaw will be wired shut, and I'll still be very weak."

"I'll file for a continuance on that basis. I'm sure the judge will grant it. Don't worry; I'll file it tomorrow."

After they hung up, Marie looked through her kitchen window. In her backyard, snow blanketed the withered remains of black-eyed Susans, wild geraniums, and astilbe plants, while ice had formed over the azalea bushes. When she had first come home from the hospital in December, family and friends had shown their support and made frequent visits. As her treatment dragged on, her friends had dropped off one by one, like soldiers on a long retreat. She realized that these people had their own lives to live and she couldn't expect them to continue to shower her with affection indefinitely. But today, she felt forgotten and very alone.

7

READY

After a lengthy third surgery, Marie came home from the hospital. However, a fourth operation loomed in six months to remove the plates on both sides of her jaw.

Lying in bed, she was exhausted after a fitful night of intermittent sleep. She'd had pain in all the familiar places: jaw, hips, throat, and head. For the third time, her jaw was wired shut for another four weeks, the wires biting into her gums once again. Each surgery had involved facial swelling and deep bruising, but the last one had caused grotesque swelling under her left eye—so much so that she looked like someone whose face had been beaten by a baseball bat. Even after Dr. Zins had inserted a drain there on the third postsurgical day and people told her that the swelling had receded, she avoided looking into a mirror.

The house was silent. She concluded that Chuck had escaped for a few hours of work and would probably be home for lunch. She turned onto her side and her right hip burned with pain, a reminder that bone had been harvested there five days earlier. Was it even worth getting out of bed today? She answered herself swiftly and decisively, remembering how an imprisoned Soviet dissident had maintained the psychological resolve to survive his ordeal. He'd treated each day as a series of simple decisions: Do you want to be sick or do you want to be well? Do you want to live or do you want to die? She would do the same. *I'm in pain. I can stay in bed or I can get out of bed. Of course, I will get out of bed.* She knew she would always choose action.

After she had blended some vegetables and fruit together for breakfast, she called the assistant prosecutor, Robert Christyson, and left a message. He called back later in the day and told her that the trial had been continued from March 31 to late in May. He had arranged for Richard Thompson to remain housed in a separate section of the jail, apart from Christopher Martin. He didn't want Martin or his friends to threaten Thompson and make him reconsider his decision to testify against his former friend.

"I really expect to be much better by May," Marie explained. "I'll wait for you to call if anything changes."

"I'll have my secretary send out a letter with the new trial date and we'll talk then," Christyson said. "I've got a meeting and have to run."

✻ ✻ ✻

Two months later, on May 25, 1988, Marie sat huddled in the back of Courtroom 17A with Carol Thornton and Brittany Kirkpatrick, awaiting the start of Christopher Martin's trial. Thornton and Kirkpatrick would join Marie as witnesses for the prosecution. After experiencing terror at the hands of Richard Thompson and Christopher Martin, the three were bonded by experiences that were both shared and unique. Each carried her own scars, but each was equally determined to do her part to put these men away. Although they'd known of each other before today, this was the first time that they were all physically present together and could talk. They had wandered into the courtroom several minutes apart, but once they saw each other, they each immediately realized who the others were.

Brittany Kirkpatrick seemed the most frightened, her body trembling under her raincoat. In her twenties, she was tall and thin with a fair Celtic complexion. Once the women had introduced themselves to each another, she was the first one to ask Marie how she was doing.

Marie's face was still puffy from the last surgery, but the arch bars that had fixed her jaw in place had been removed several months ago. She'd worked tirelessly for the past six weeks to increase her jaw opening from six millimeters to nineteen. Unable to chew, she was still on a liquid diet.

As she pondered Brittany's question, Marie didn't know how much to disclose about her limitations. Due to nerve damage, her tongue no longer tasted foods except at its base. As a result, she had lost much of her sense of taste. Because nerve damage had also eliminated feeling in her chin, lower lip, and lower gum, she could not sense when food or saliva escaped from her mouth and rolled down her chin. She could no longer move her jaw forward or backward and could move it only slightly in a lateral motion, all of which made it unlikely that she would ever be able to chew hard foods like apples or hard-crusted bread again. Always proud of her ability to communicate, Marie was embarrassed that she couldn't enunciate all sounds and had to speak more slowly.

"I'm just glad to be alive," Marie said. "I've got some problems with my jaw and mouth, but I'll work around them. How are you, Brittany?"

Brittany took a deep breath and whispered, "I'm fine as long as I don't think about that night, but when I do . . ." Her words trailed off. Marie and Carol nodded their understanding, and Carol took Brittany's hand. The three sat in silence for a few moments.

"I'm okay," Carol suddenly volunteered. "I don't want any woman to go through what I experienced. I want these guys put away for a long time."

Just then, the deputies escorted Christopher Martin into the courtroom. If he had not been scowling, Martin would have been nice looking. He was a black male, about twenty years old, six feet tall, and of medium build. He had exchanged his orange jail jumpsuit for jeans and a black-and-gray sweatshirt. He swaggered as he entered, then turned and stared at the three women in an obvious attempt to intimidate them. His look conveyed his contempt for the women, and each knew that if he was acquitted, they would always live in fear of his reprisal. If he was set free, they would never feel safe, ever.

"Christyson told me he's got alibi witnesses," Carol Thornton whispered. "He's claiming that he was at work or something when these crimes occurred. He's bringing in a co-employee."

Marie and Brittany flinched at the news and looked at one another. Thornton continued, "He's waiving a jury trial and is going to let Judge Character decide if he's guilty or not."

Marie was impressed that Thornton had all of the inside information and waited for her to disclose more, but she did not.

"Why would he waive his right to a jury trial?" Marie asked. As an attorney, she knew that a defendant normally fared better with a jury than with a judge; judges, after years of experience evaluating criminal defendants, were much more skeptical of defendants' stories.

"I wonder if it's because the judge is black," Brittany said.

Again, it was Thornton who spoke up. "Governor Celeste just appointed him to a vacant judgeship last year. I've talked to some attorney friends, and he doesn't have a track record yet. I do know that he is a former law partner of Carl Stokes and Louis Stokes."

She's obviously done her homework, Marie thought. When Marie had first arrived in Cleveland, she'd worked on Carl Stokes's mayoral campaign, stuffing envelopes and helping to register black voters. She'd been very excited when Stokes had won, becoming the first African American to be elected the mayor of a major U.S. city. She knew that his brother, Congressman Louis Stokes, was a fixture in the U.S. House of Representatives.

"What else do you know about him?" Marie asked.

"Not much. I think my friends said he'd graduated from the University of Michigan Law School."

Marie was impressed—the U of M Law School was one of the top ten law schools in the country. Character was no doubt very smart.

When the women looked up, they noticed that the judge had entered the courtroom. Judge Character looked to be in his late fifties and wore a serious, if not stern, expression this morning. Wearing a starched white shirt and gray tie under his robe, he looked all business. He brushed his hand against his receding hairline and adjusted his large-framed glasses. His right hand came to rest under his chin, and he peered down at the two attorneys, who were putting trial motions on the record. Suddenly, the judge looked up and was staring at the three women in the back of the courtroom. As the women listened to the defense attorney, Timothy Gauntner, they realized that they were the subject of Gauntner's motion.

"There are three witnesses in the back of the courtroom who will be called to identify my client as the man who robbed them. They have watched as my client has come into the courtroom. They are obviously talking with one another. They should have been separated and kept out of the courtroom until each was called to testify. Any identification that they make now will be tainted by this, and I move for a dismissal of all charges."

The trio shuddered in astonishment. Had they just irrevocably prejudiced the state's case against Martin? Why hadn't the prosecutor told them to stay out of the courtroom?

If the motion had startled Assistant Prosecutor Christyson, he didn't show it. "Your Honor, months before this trial, all of these witnesses identified the defendant from in-person lineups and photo IDs. Their identifications are in no way tainted by what they have observed when the defendant was brought into the courtroom today."

Marie knew that the prosecutor's claim was not entirely correct. She had never identified Christopher Martin in any way because she had never seen him or his face. Had the prosecutor forgotten that? Did he expect her to identify him when she testified?

"Motion for dismissal overruled," Judge Character snapped. "However, I am assuming that one of the attorneys will make a motion for the separation of witnesses."

"Yes," both attorneys responded in unison.

"All right, ladies in the back and any other witnesses, if you are a witness for the prosecution or the defense, you must leave the courtroom now and wait in the hallway until you are called. Once you have testified, you may remain in the courtroom to listen to the remainder of the trial—that is, if you so choose."

The three women stood up and walked out into the hall. After confirming that Martin had knowingly waived his right to a jury trial, Judge Character asked the attorneys to give opening statements. Because the judge was familiar with the case, both men kept their remarks short.

Christyson maintained that Martin and "another man" had lain in wait for single women at the menu boards of fast-food restaurants and stuck a gun through the car window to force entry and compel the women to withdraw money from ATMs. The men robbed two women this way, but with a third, things did not go as planned and the victim had been shot through the face. The prosecution would prove that Martin was one of the two men involved in all three crimes.

Gauntner, the defense attorney, limited his opening to two sentences. He told the court that his client had not been present at any of the robberies and had an alibi on the nights of the crimes.

The trial would be a quick one. Neither attorney intended to do anything more than paint with a broad brush. For the Kirkpatrick and Thornton robberies, the prosecutor would rely almost entirely upon the victims' positive identification of Martin. For Marie, he would build his case with the testimony of the codefendant, Richard Thompson.

The defense would counter with alibi witnesses. The judge would be called upon to evaluate the certainty of the prosecution's identification witnesses, assess the strength of their memories, and then weigh them against the defendant's alibi witnesses. In gauging the alibi witnesses, the judge would ask himself a series of questions: What was the alibi witness's relationship to the defendant, how credible was the alibi witness, and was the witness's testimony consistent with other evidence in the case? If they told a plausible story, reasonable doubt would follow.

Both lawyers knew that dramatic questioning and emotional oratory were not likely to sway the judge. In the final analysis, this case rested in the hands of Brittany Kirkpatrick, Carol Thornton, Marie, and Richard Thompson. If they faltered, Martin would likely escape a conviction.

The prosecutor called Brittany Kirkpatrick as the state's first witness. After being sworn, Ms. Kirkpatrick spoke so quietly that the judge asked her to speak up, explaining that he could not hear her over the hum of the air-conditioning. Despite this request, Kirkpatrick's voice quavered and was barely loud enough for anyone other than the nearby court reporter to hear her. She explained that she had been with friends in the Flats on October 24, 1987, and was returning home at around 11:30 that night when she decided to order some food from the Burger King drive-thru. Because three cars were in front of her at the menu board, she felt secure. However, after she placed her order, two men came running toward the car.

Her voice shook as she recalled the details. "One man had a gun. I had a two-door car and he yelled, 'Move over, bitch, and let me in.' I was really scared, but finally I got the door open, and he got into the backseat and stuck the gun at my neck. I was too nervous to open the passenger door for the other guy, and finally the guy in the backseat opened it and the other man got in. They told me to drive out and not look suspicious or else they would shoot me."

Kirkpatrick closed her eyes as she remembered the encounter. She held her hands tightly in her lap and looked down at them, her face accidentally brushing the microphone in the process.

"Go on. What happened next?"

"I was really scared. I kept saying, 'Don't hurt me. Don't hurt me.' I was crying, and the one in the back told me to get out my asset card and drive to an ATM. When I told him I didn't have one, he took my purse and rummaged through it. He told the other guy that he'd found my wallet, but there wasn't much in it. I kept telling them to take my money, and I begged them not to hurt me and let me out."

"Did they?"

"No, not at this point. The one guy asked me if I had any jewelry. He started feeling around my neck, but I was wearing a high-collared dress and the jewelry was underneath it so he didn't find it. He asked about rings and couldn't find one. They told me to keep driving and not look suspicious. I was sure they were going to kill me."

Kirkpatrick paused for a moment to regain her composure and then glanced at the judge, who was listening intently.

She continued, "The guy beside me said, 'Just let her out.' But the other guy, the man behind me, said, 'No way.' They argued back and forth and finally I stopped the car. The guy in the passenger seat got out and came to my door—like he was going to get in and drive—and he wanted me to move over to the passenger seat. They kept arguing about what to do with me. Finally, they agreed to let me go and take my car. One of them said, 'If you watch us drive away, we'll shoot you.' So I turned away from my car—this was at Ninety-Third and Chester—and I didn't look in their direction."

"Is either of those two men in the courtroom today?"

"Yes, one of them is. He's the man in the gray-and-black sweatshirt."

The prosecutor said, "Let the record reflect that the witness has identified Christopher Martin.

"What about the other man?" the prosecutor asked. As soon as he'd asked the question, he realized that he'd made a mistake. From prior meetings with Kirkpatrick, Christyson knew that she would describe the other man as black and shorter than Martin. This was a problem; Thompson was six inches taller than Martin. The state contended that both men had committed all three robberies. If Kirkpatrick was wrong in her description of Thompson, how accurate was her identification of Martin?

"The other man was black and shorter. I'm sure I could identify him if I was shown a picture of him."

Intent on moving on, Christyson asked his next question quickly and changed the subject. "Where was Martin seated in the car?"

Kirkpatrick squirmed in her chair and then looked helplessly at the prosecutor. "As I told you, I don't know. I was so frightened; I just can't remember this. All I can say is that Mr. Martin was one of the two men."

"Did you pick him out of a lineup?"

"Yes. I first looked at five or six Polaroid photos of various suspects, and I picked him out immediately. The same was true when I went down to the Justice Center and viewed a lineup of five or six men."

"Any question that Mr. Martin was one of the two men?"

"No."

Kirkpatrick was unable to identify the gun used in the Grossman robbery as the one that was held to her head. She did confirm that money was taken from her purse and that her Visa card was missing.

On cross-examination, Gauntner asked Kirkpatrick if she had consumed any alcoholic beverages in the Flats that night. She denied that she had.

"So you had been at Shooters and Coconuts that night and had nothing alcoholic to drink?"

"Yes, that's what I said."

Kirkpatrick's direct testimony had exposed lapses in her memory, and Gauntner planned to exploit them. He confirmed that she was unable to say where her purse had been located in the car or whether she or the man in the front seat had handed it to the man in the backseat.

"You were very frightened, weren't you?"

"Yes."

"And because you were frightened, you have gaps in your memory?"

"Yes, there are things I can't remember."

"You've said that you are not certain whether Christopher Martin was in the front seat or the backseat?"

"That's correct."

Gauntner could feel the momentum swinging in his favor. Kirkpatrick appeared to be a shaky witness, perhaps pushed by the police and prosecution to make an identification that she would now recant if pressed. In a very casual tone, he asked, "And you are *not* one hundred percent certain that Christopher Martin was in the car with you that night?"

"Could you repeat the question, please?" Kirkpatrick responded. The prosecutor stiffened, fearing that his witness was about to cave.

"And you are *not* one hundred percent certain that Christopher Martin was in the car with you that night?" Gauntner repeated.

"I know he was. I'm one hundred percent certain he was in the car that night," Kirkpatrick answered.

"You're pretty sure?" Gauntner asked, seeking to find some soft spot in the identification.

"I'm one hundred percent sure he was in the car."

Gauntner's shoulders slumped for just a moment. He forced an exasperated expression and shook his head, trying to convey his disbelief to the judge. "Thank you, Ms. Kirkpatrick. No further questions," he said.

"Any redirect, Mr. Christyson?" the judge asked.

"No, your honor," Christyson answered quickly. His witness had faltered and then righted herself, and he would not prolong her time on the stand or give the defense attorney a second chance to question her.

Christyson was relieved that Gauntner had not exploited Kirkpatrick's faulty description of the codefendant, Richard Thompson. What if Gauntner had asked: Are you *as certain* of your identification of my client as you are about the height of his accomplice? If she had said that she was, the judge would no longer be able to trust her identification of Martin.

Unless the defendant presented a compelling alibi witness, the assistant prosecutor felt confident that, at the very least, Martin would be convicted of robbing and abducting Kirkpatrick. He could now move on to the next part of his case—the robbery and kidnapping of Carol Thornton.

The prosecutor believed that Carol Thornton would be an effective witness. She'd impressed him as bright, articulate, and confident, but how many times had he felt the same way about other witnesses, only to be disappointed at trial? Like Kirkpatrick, Thornton was a young woman in her twenties. As she approached the witness stand, she walked briskly, her suit jacket billowing behind her. Her quick pace puzzled the prosecutor; she was either extremely self-assured or scared out of her mind. When she reached her seat and sat down, she revealed the answer. Thornton looked directly at the defendant and continued to focus on him until Christyson asked his first question.

Thornton told the judge that she had been at the menu board at the Popeyes at 8210 Euclid Avenue around 11 p.m. when a man approached the driver's-side door. At first she couldn't understand what he was asking, and he repeated his message several times before she understood that he wanted her to unlock the door and let him in. When she didn't, he pulled a gun from his pocket and pointed it at her neck. She unlocked the door, moved over, and watched as the man got behind the steering wheel. He told her to unlock all the doors, and another person got into the car and sat directly behind her. The first man handed the gun to his accomplice, and he held it at her neck.

They asked her for an "asset card," and she told them that she didn't have one. She then realized that they wanted any bank card, not a specific one, and she told them that she had a bank card for Bank One. They drove around, somewhat aimlessly, as they discussed where the closest Bank One ATM was located. The trip was prolonged because the driver kept making wrong turns until they finally arrived at an ATM at Cedar and Fairmont. The two men then argued about who would accompany her to the ATM. The man sitting in the backseat didn't want to be seen because he had a gun and there were people on the nearby sidewalks. The driver told him to put the gun in his pocket and accompany Thornton, which he did.

He then followed her to the ATM and directed her to withdraw her maximum limit. She withdrew $250, and then he asked her to withdraw another $50. Each time the machine spit out the cash, he reached over her shoulder and grabbed the money. When they were through, he told her that she was to walk in front of him to the car and get back in. As a result, she did not see his face. When all three were back in the car, the men discussed whether or not they would drive back to Cedar Road and catch a bus.

"I strongly encouraged them to do that, to allow me to drop them off at a bus stop, but then they decided that they would keep the car and let me out at Fairhill near Baldwin," she said, completing her account of the ordeal.

After listening to her long narrative, Christyson shifted to the crux of her testimony. "Miss Thornton, can you describe these men?"

"Yes."

"Would you, please?"

"The first man who approached me was of average height, not tall. He was young, well dressed, casually dressed, but clean. He was a reasonably attractive young man. I think the reason I had trouble understanding him at first is that he did not look particularly menacing. Subsequently he did look menacing as he got more impatient with me and I recognized that he had a gun.

"The other fellow, I never really saw his face clearly. I saw his body. He was very tall and slender, and he was also casually dressed."

Christyson was pleased with Thornton's testimony. When Thompson testified later, the tall accomplice would fit perfectly with Thornton's description.

"The first man you described, what did his role seem to be in all of this?" the prosecutor asked.

"He did the talking. My impression was that he was the leader."

"Objection," Gauntner said.

"Sustained."

"Was he the driver?"

"Yes."

"Do you see that man in the courtroom today?"

"Yes, I do," Carol Thornton said, pointing to Christopher Martin. "He is sitting right there and is wearing a gray-and-black sweatshirt."

"One final question, Miss Thornton: At any time did either man threaten you?"

"Yes. They said that if I did not cooperate, they would be forced to hurt me and they didn't want to do that."

As Gauntner rose to cross-examine, he smelled a setup. How was it that both women could positively identify his client but could not identify Thompson, the man who had turned state's evidence? He would prod and probe, determined to show that something was amiss. He hoped that Thornton, like Kirkpatrick, would have gaps in her memory too.

The defense attorney decided to test the witness on many fine points, hoping that she'd be unable to remember certain details and, in the process, cast doubt on her identification of his client. But Thornton remembered the specifics. She knew that November 14 was a Saturday, that she was coming from home, that Popeyes was on the south side of Euclid Avenue, that the cool evening temperature required her to wear a sweater, that the defendant was wearing a jacket with brown corduroy pants, that there was bright lighting in the Popeyes parking lot, that there were two cars in front of her in the drive-thru, and that her purse was located on the floor next to her. She did not hesitate with her answers, and Gauntner was about to give up with this line of questioning when the witness made a small mistake.

"How long did you drive around with these two men in the car?" Gauntner asked, knowing that witnesses routinely overestimated periods of time.

"Probably an hour to an hour and a half," Thornton replied. The assistant prosecutor grimaced as he heard the answer.

How could Thornton have been in the car with Thompson for over an hour and *not* be able to identify him? Gauntner would file that question away for later.

The defense attorney continued to attack the reliability of the identification. Thornton testified that the day following the incident, she looked at photos of suspects but was unable to identify any as her assailants. Over a month later, she returned to the Justice Center to view a lineup of six men. At that time, she identified Martin as the man who approached the car and forced his way in.

"Has it ever happened to you that you are walking around somewhere and you see somebody that you think you know and you say hello and it turns out they are not that person?"

"Objection."

"Overruled."

"Certainly," Thornton replied, undaunted by the question.

"That certainly happens to all of us, does it not?" Gauntner replied. He was reverting to stock cross-examination questions that, although they were marginally persuasive to a jury, would not likely impress a judge. "Perhaps somebody that you might feel that you know pretty well, and it turns out that it is somebody else."

"Probably," Thornton answered, a bit warier this time.

"And this happens when you are relaxed?"

"I suppose."

"But on November fourteenth—you've indicated that this experience was worse than a nightmare. Right?"

"Yes."

"And you're trying to make an identification when it is night and dark outside?"

Thornton could see where the defense attorney was going, and she did not like it. "Wait a minute; I said the parking lot was well lit."

Ignoring her, Gauntner said, "You mean there would be streetlights; is that what you mean?"

"Well, yes, once we got out of the parking lot."

Gauntner turned away from the witness, his back facing her now. "If I were to turn around, would you be able to tell me the color of my necktie?"

"Objection, Your Honor," Christyson yelled.

"She may answer," the judge replied.

Repeating his question, the prosecutor asked, "But you could not, is that correct?"

"No, I can't tell you what color it is, but may I elaborate?"

"No, you can't," the judge answered.

Gauntner was ready to return to Thornton's inability to identify the accomplice, Thompson.

"You're telling us with all the things that went on with these two men, you can't identify the tall man?"

"I can't."

"He got out of the car with you?"

"Yes."

"He was with you for about five minutes as you withdrew money from the ATM?"

"Yes."

"And you can't recognize that person?"

"He was behind me," Thornton said, her voice showing irritation for the first time.

"Who got out of the car first, you or him?"

"I did."

"And you didn't look behind you when he got out?"

"No."

Feigning disbelief, Gauntner concluded, "And you were in this person's company for over an hour?"

"Uh-huh," Thornton replied. She looked at the judge, trying to discern whether he was impressed by this line of questioning. The judge looked tired, his right hand supporting his chin.

"No further questions," Gauntner said.

Christyson was not sure if his opponent's cross-examination had scored any points with Judge Character, but he decided to regain some momentum by returning the witness to her core testimony.

"Any redirect, Mr. Christyson?"

"Yes, Your Honor." Back at the podium, he asked, "Miss Thornton, did you pick anybody out of the police lineup?"

"Yes, I did."

"Did the police tell you who that was?"

"Yes, after I left."

"And who was it?"

"It was the defendant, Christopher Martin."

"Was Christopher Martin one of the men who forced his way into your car that night?"

"Yes, he was."

"Did Christopher Martin hold a gun on you that night?"

"Yes, he did."

"Did Christopher Martin steal your car that night?"

"Yes, he did."

"Did Christopher Martin threaten to shoot you if you didn't cooperate?"

"Yes, he did."

The prosecutor had no further questions, and Gauntner declined to cross-examine the witness again.

The judge weighed in. "Unfortunately, we got a delayed start today because of several sentencings. It is late right now, and because the next witness may take some time, we will recess this trial until 10 a.m. tomorrow morning."

Out in the hall, Marie hoped that she would be allowed to testify before the judge adjourned for the day. For the past three hours, she'd alternated between sitting on an uncomfortable wooden bench and pacing the long hall. When Christyson told her that she would have to appear again tomorrow, she tried not to show her disappointment.

"Okay. See you tomorrow." What else could she say?

A few minutes later, Brittany Kirkpatrick and Carol Thornton filed out of the courtroom and joined Marie as she waited for the elevator. Both were relieved, but Thornton was angry, convinced that the defense attorney's tactics had compromised the force of her testimony.

"You were very good," said Kirkpatrick, who had remained in the courtroom after she'd finished her testimony. "I thought his questions were stupid. Who cares if you couldn't identify the color of his tie?"

"Marie, be careful with that Gauntner. He'll try to twist whatever you say," Thornton sputtered.

"I'm sure you were fine," Marie answered. She wasn't worried about the defense attorney. She'd spent the past fifteen years dealing with attorneys, and she doubted that any court-appointed defense attorney could trip her up if she listened carefully to his questions. "Are either of you coming back tomorrow?"

Both said that they wanted to but could not. They had already taken significant time off work to meet with the prosecutor and then attend the trial's first day. Any more time off and they would be testing the patience of their employers.

After the elevator deposited them on the ground floor, they walked out of the Justice Center together.

"Good luck tomorrow," Kirkpatrick told her.

"You'll do fine," Thornton added.

"If I get a good night's sleep, I will," Marie answered as they went their separate ways.

8

TESTIMONY

For the entire day, Marie had waited anxiously to testify. The effort had exhausted her, and that evening she slept soundly. Eight miles away at the Cuyahoga County Jail, Richard Thompson did not fare as well. That night he'd received a threat from another inmate. "You know what happens to snitches," the man had said.

Still wide awake at 3 a.m., Thompson's long legs extended out from his bed as he turned toward the wall. Anyone who called him a snitch didn't know the entire story. Thompson had convinced himself that Christopher Martin had betrayed him on the night of the shooting. Why hadn't the police tested Martin for gunshot residue? For Thompson, the answer was simple. When questioned by the detectives, Martin must have identified him as the shooter. Martin was the real informant, not him, and he was justified in evening the score.

However, Thompson's flimsy reasoning didn't make any sense. Martin had steadfastly denied that he was present at any of the robberies. To identify Thompson as the shooter would have been an admission that he was present. Nevertheless, Thompson clung to this misguided conclusion.

As sleep eluded him, he also thought about the plea deal and how stupid he'd been to agree to it. What had the prosecutor given him in the bargain? Nothing. They'd dropped charges connected to two robberies where no one could identify him as being present. They couldn't have convicted him of those crimes anyway. Why did he accept the deal? Was it out of fear? Was it out of guilt over what he'd done? He wasn't sure.

From the moment the police had forced him to pull over his car, he'd been scared. When they'd told him that the woman at Burger King had been shot in the head, he'd been terrified. He'd cried at the scene. Yes, big, tough Richard Thompson had lost it and sobbed like a schoolkid. He realized that his life, as he knew it, was over. If this woman died, he'd get the death penalty. If she lived, he'd go to prison for a long time. The world was crashing down around him in a way that he'd never imagined.

But that wasn't the only reason he'd broken down. He'd cried because he'd understood the enormity of what he'd just done. This was not a petty robbery—a game to get money for drugs. He'd injured someone, perhaps killed a complete stranger, a woman with a husband and maybe children. He knew better, and he was ashamed. He was humiliated not only for himself but for his parents, who were good people who had always provided for him. He'd let his whole family down.

He stared at the cell walls, then at the sink and toilet. This was his future now. He'd committed the crime, and he'd been caught. The victim had identified him. He'd had gunshot residue on his right hand. He'd been found with her purse and credit cards in his car. There was no way out, and he wanted to be done with it.

He'd tell the truth—well, mainly the truth. He'd claim that Martin was the leader, the really bad one. He'd be the follower, the clumsy dupe who'd allowed the gun to discharge. He'd exaggerate his drug use—emphasize the coke, not just the weed. That would make him seem less culpable. But the main part would be true. Martin had been there and was just as guilty as he was. He'd testify as promised and accept his punishment.

* * *

Accompanied by Chuck and Joe, Marie arrived at the courtroom at 9:30, a half an hour before the trial was to begin its second day. Just in case Christyson wanted to talk to her prior to her testimony, she waited on a bench in the hallway, while her son and husband took seats in the courtroom. Five minutes before ten, Christyson emerged from the elevator. He walked over to Marie and told her that he would call her first and that she should remain in the hallway until the bailiff came for her.

"Do you want to go over the key questions with me?"

"I don't think that's necessary. You'll know the answers to everything I ask."

Christyson knew that Marie, unlike the other two women, was not critical to this part of the case. Thompson had pled guilty to the charges stemming from Marie's incident yesterday morning. That was a done deal. As for the case involving Martin, Marie had never seen him at the scene. During her testimony, she merely needed to set the stage for the crime and explain what had happened to her. The case against Martin would rise or fall on Thompson's credibility when he fingered Martin as his partner.

When the bailiff brought Marie into the courtroom, she saw her two family members sitting in the back row. The defendant, Christopher Martin, turned his head, and his eyes followed her from the back of the courtroom until she reached the witness chair. His threatening glare was meant to intimidate her, but Marie barely glanced at him. Her focus was on the judge as she took her seat. As a lawyer, she knew it was important for a witness to maintain eye contact with the trier of fact—in this case, the judge.

The prosecutor's first few questions allowed her to set the crime scene and explain why she was at the Burger King that evening around 6:30 p.m. Freed from bands and wires, Marie's jaw opened sufficiently to allow her to speak clearly and slowly. Keeping her voice loud, she directed her answers to the judge. She explained how Richard Thompson had approached the car and stuck a gun into the open window and how she had attempted to give him her purse. During the encounter, the gunman had periodically looked over the roof of the car.

"I got the feeling that he was looking at someone else," Marie said.

"Objection."

"Sustained as to what you were feeling," the judge ruled.

Marie told the judge that she attempted to get out of the car and turn the vehicle over to her assailant. Instead, the man placed his hand on her seat and began to push it forward, trying to force his way into the backseat. When she realized that he wanted in, she pressed down on the accelerator to get away.

"And what happened next, Mrs. Grossman?"

"He shot me in the head."

"And he shot you where exactly?"

"He shot me right here. The bullet went in here, and it came out here," she said, pointing to the two scars on her cheeks.

Not more than eight feet away, Judge Character focused on Marie's cheeks, and he, too, studied where the bullet had entered and exited. The judge switched his gaze to the defendant, scowled, and raised his eyebrows, leaving no doubt that he was upset by both Martin and Thompson. They'd inflicted needless agony upon this woman, a lawyer like himself.

Christyson caught the judge's reaction. This was exactly the response he'd hoped for. These punks had terrified women like this for months, and he was confident that Judge Character was getting the message.

To leave no doubt about the seriousness of her injuries, the prosecutor asked Marie about her three surgeries, the length of her hospitalizations, and her permanent impairments. He then laid the foundation for the next part of his case, demonstrating that Richard Thompson was the shooter.

"Showing you what has been marked as State's Exhibits Three, Four, Five, Six, and Seven, could you tell us what those are?"

"These are pictures of young men."

"Are they the pictures that were shown to you by the detective?"

"They were pictures like this. The only one I remember for sure is the one I identified, which is the second picture here."

"Were you eventually told that person's name?"

"Yes, I was told that this is a photograph of Richard Thompson."

Upon further questioning, Marie admitted that she did not see anyone else at the scene. She observed Thompson continually looking over the top of her car, but she never took her eyes off of him and did not know what he was looking at. When the defense attorney opted not to cross-examine her, the stage was set for Richard Thompson to implicate Martin in the robbery.

Marie stepped down and joined her family in the back row. Chuck told her that she had done very well. "I really wasn't that nervous," she whispered back.

A sheriff's deputy ushered Richard Thompson into the courtroom. The lean, pencil-thin teenager was wearing his orange jail jumpsuit and walked slowly to the front of the courtroom, where the bailiff administered the oath. Thompson's voice was barely audible when he answered yes to the bailiff's question.

Gauntner objected as soon as Thompson sat down in the witness chair. "It is my understanding that Mr. Thompson is going to testify that he did not act alone on December 11, 1987, but was engaged in criminal behavior with my client. Mrs. Grossman never identified my client as being at the scene. If Mr. Thompson is allowed to testify, this would be the uncorroborated testimony of a codefendant, which should be excluded under the criminal rules."

"I don't understand the basis of the objection," Christyson said.

Marie listened intently. Although not schooled in criminal law, she understood immediately that the defense attorney's argument, if correct, would derail the prosecution's case against Martin for the shooting at Burger King. At that realization, she felt both despair and guilt, as if her inability to identify Martin were somehow her fault. She hoped that Christyson was not caught by surprise and could counter this.

The judge weighed in. "The current criminal rules allow for the uncorroborated testimony of a coconspirator or of an aider and abettor. So the objection will be overruled."

Christyson nodded his approval and added, "A coconspirator's testimony is simply to be treated as that of any other witness."

Marie looked at Chuck, who squeezed her hand. Thompson would get his chance to implicate Martin. Marie stared at Judge Character, admiring his ability to make quick decisions and his detailed knowledge of criminal law.

Thompson sat slouched in the witness chair, his back stooped in order to get his mouth near the microphone that had been set for the much shorter Marie. After his first answer, Gauntner complained that he could not hear Thompson. The bailiff stepped down, walked over to the witness, moved the microphone higher, and told Thompson to speak into it. Thompson sat up straighter and leaned toward the microphone.

Thompson told the judge that he and Martin had been together the entire day getting high. When it got dark, they decided to rob someone in order to get money to buy more "cheeb" and cocaine. Thompson did not indicate how they each got to the nearby Burger King, but he claimed that once there, they waited in Martin's car for a woman to use the drive-thru.

Thompson did not disclose that they'd driven together to the Burger King in his own blue Chevy. After the shooting, two eyewitnesses had told police that the pair had arrived in a blue Chevy with license plate number 736PUH, a car that the police quickly found was registered to Richard Thompson.

"Whose plan was it, or who decided that you should wait at Burger King for somebody to rob?"

"Christopher's."

"Did you have a weapon?"

"Christopher had the gun, but he gave it to me."

Thompson kept his eyes locked on the prosecutor, never venturing a glance at Martin. Thompson had good reason to avoid looking at his codefendant. The gun belonged to both of them. He'd spotted it at the home of a neighbor, and several months earlier, he and Martin had broken into the house and stolen it together. Since then, the two had robbed approximately a dozen people with that gun, and each had carried it on him from time to time. Thompson's assertion that Martin was the "mastermind" behind the Burger King job was also a stretch.

Thompson testified that after about an hour's wait in the parking lot, they spotted Mrs. Grossman's car approaching the drive-thru.

"I got out of the car, and Christopher stood at the car. He had already told me what to do and what not to," Thompson explained. Sensing that he needed to distance himself from Martin, Thompson added, "This was my first time doing this." Fifteen feet away, Martin sneered in disbelief, bringing a cautionary glance from his attorney.

"Tell us what happened next," the prosecutor urged.

"He said that he would stand by the car and watch. I asked her to— he told me to ask her to slide over, and I asked her to slide over, and she paused for a second because she was scared. I was scared, too. And then she threw her purse at me, and when she threw her purse at me, she pulled off, and when she pulled off, the car hit the gun—the car door hit the gun and the gun went off."

Marie pursed her lips. Not only was Thompson implicating Martin, but Marie could see that he was also whitewashing his own role in discharging the gun. She hadn't thrown her purse at him. Instead, she'd slowly placed it on the window ledge. It was Thompson who'd failed to take it and let it drop to the ground. She'd also offered her car keys to him and been refused. Looking at Chuck, she shook her head in disbelief.

Thompson went on. "After the gun went off and she drove the car forward, I grabbed the purse real fast. Me and him split up and ran in different directions." Again, Thompson did not relate the complete story. Witnesses had seen him return to the parking lot ten minutes after he ran away and retrieve his blue Chevy.

"We eventually met on the street. When we did, Chris asked me, 'What happened?' and I said, 'The gun went off.' I was panicking. I said, 'I hope I didn't shoot her. I hope I didn't shoot her.'"

According to Thompson, the two returned to Christopher's house, where they split the money that they'd found in the purse. From there, Thompson claimed that they'd walked to his house in order to get his car. He said that they were driving around when a police cruiser passed them, put on its flashers, and pulled them over for making a wide right turn.

"They put us in the back of the cruiser while one of the cops searched my car. He came back with Chris's gun and some of the woman's credit cards. They arrested us after that."

Christyson decided that he had established all that he could with Thompson and ended his questioning. On cross-examination, Gauntner confirmed that his client never approached the Grossman car but stood by his own vehicle.

"Let's be clear: everything you did that day was what you wanted to do?" Gauntner asked.

"Well, not really. Like I said, we was both high on cocaine and stuff. He asked me to do it. I didn't want to do it, but he kept asking me. Finally, he said, 'Do you want to get some more cocaine?'" The witness shook his head and then continued, "Because you see, we do it every day. It's a bad habit."

Gauntner probed the plea bargain, establishing that in exchange for Thompson's testimony against his client, the prosecutor had dropped two robbery charges against him.

"And your testimony about Christopher Martin is a lie, isn't it?"

"No."

"You are doing this to help yourself, right?"

"No."

"To save your own skin?"

"No."

"You don't deny that you got a bargain from the prosecutor's office, do you?"

"No, I don't deny that."

On this perceived high note, the defense attorney concluded his cross-examination.

"What did you think of his testimony?" Chuck whispered to Marie.

"I guess he did okay," she answered tersely, still rankled by Thompson's claim that she'd thrown her purse at him.

Christyson next called two of the investigating officers to connect the defendants to the cars at the scene and the things found in them. Captain David Good, an eighteen-year veteran, told the judge that he and Lieutenant Moon arrived at the scene and received descriptions of the suspects and their cars from the first responding patrol officers around 7 p.m. The witnesses said that the men had been inside two cars, a blue Chevy and a maroon Camaro. They'd written down the plates for the Chevy when it was driven away, but the maroon Camaro was still in the Burger King parking lot. A quick check of the plate number disclosed that the blue Chevy was registered to Richard Thompson.

Armed with this knowledge, the police officers decided to drive over to Thompson's house. On their way, they spotted his car coming in the opposite direction. Lieutenant Moon, who was driving, executed a U-turn and put on the cruiser's flashers, and the Chevy pulled over in response. Good and Moon approached the car, ordered the men out, frisked them, told them that they were under arrest for aggravated robbery, handcuffed them, and put them in the cruiser. Moon searched the Chevy and found the gun, Marie Grossman's driver's license, and her bank card under the front passenger seat.

Marie sensed that the prosecutor's case was gaining strength as he scored point after point with little opposition from his counterpart. She nudged Chuck and whispered, "I think things are going really well."

Detective Joseph Nowak entered the courtroom as the next witness. He seemed to be wearing the same brown sport coat that he'd worn to the hospital. Nowak testified that he was present when the suspects' gun, a Charter Arms .38-caliber revolver, was tested for operability. The prosecution was required to show that the defendant's gun actually worked in order to invoke a longer mandatory prison time for the crime. With this condition satisfied, the prosecution rested.

"Is that all he's going to ask him?" Chuck whispered to Marie. "What about the women in the halfway house and what they told him?"

"I don't know. I'm guessing that the prosecutor is feeling very confident right now and wants to move things along," Marie responded.

Just then, the prosecutor stood up and told the judge that the state was resting, subject to the introduction of its exhibits.

Marie and Chuck exchanged surprised glances. It was time for the noon recess, and when they returned, they would learn how Timothy Gauntner intended to defend his client.

9

THE COURT DECIDES

After lunch, the judge asked Gauntner to proceed with his client's defense. Gauntner had alibi witnesses for two of the robberies, the ones involving Thornton and Grossman, but not Kirkpatrick's. He would lead with his strongest witness, Charles Winter, a twenty-six-year-old black man who was a friend of Martin's sister and mother. Winter had a neat appearance, wearing black dress pants and a long-sleeved blue shirt. He nodded slightly to the defendant when he sat down in the witness chair.

Winter told the judge that he knew Martin from the neighborhood. Although he was employed as a shuttle driver at the Hopkins International Airport Budget Rent a Car, he also did side jobs and employed Martin and other neighborhood kids during the summer. He explained, "I help kids during the summer by getting them jobs—painting and cutting grass and stuff like that. I try to help out in the community."

Winter told the judge that on the night of the Popeyes robbery, Martin was working for him at his uncle's bar, the Togo Suite, from 9:30 p.m. until 3 a.m. A security guard had called off sick at the last minute, and Winter had asked Martin to take his place. Winter drove Martin to the club, where Winter worked inside and Martin stayed outside in the parking lot, making sure that no one broke into the customers' cars.

"You were there that entire time, 9:30 p.m. until 3 a.m.?"

"Yes."

"How about Christopher Martin, was he there the entire time?"

"Yes."

"I have no further questions."

Marie looked at Chuck. She raised her eyebrows and whispered, "He was kind of a good witness, don't you think?"

"I'm not convinced by it, if that's what you're asking me," Chuck replied.

"You don't have to be convinced. His testimony just has to raise some doubt, you know, reasonable doubt, and he may have done that," she whispered back.

Christyson looked worried for the first time. Winter seemed like a believable witness, and now he regretted that he hadn't sent an investigator to talk to him. He had nothing to go on and would have to cross-examine him blindly. This was dangerous, but it was something that an overworked prosecutor was frequently forced to do. How many times had he violated the cardinal rule of cross-examination—never ask a question to which you don't know the answer? Sometimes he struck gold, and other times, well, he got burned. It was always a gamble.

He had several options. The safest approach was to develop the friendship between Winters and the Martin family and use that to discredit him, but he doubted that would do enough damage. In his experience, alibi witnesses fit into one of three groups: those who told the truth, those who lied, and those who were sincere but were mistaken. He guessed Winter fit into the last category. He would probe and try to find the mistake.

After asking some preliminary questions, Christyson searched for the weak link in Winter's testimony.

"You worked inside the club that night?"

"Yes."

"What did you do inside?"

"I picked up glasses and washed dishes. Sometimes greeted people when they came in."

"Martin was outside, watching cars in the parking lot, right?"

"Yes."

Christyson developed that Winter had seen Martin off and on throughout the night. The issue was whether any of these gaps were long enough to allow Martin to join Thompson at Popeyes and rob Carol Thornton.

"You didn't see him all the time then?"

"Right."

"There could have been gaps of an hour or so when you didn't see him?" the prosecutor ventured.

"Possibly."

Christyson needed more. After the witness told him that the club was located at Fairhill and Cedar, the prosecutor asked him how long it would take to drive to Popeyes at Eighty-Second and Euclid Avenue from there. Winters thought it would take about ten or fifteen minutes.

Marie wanted Christyson to continue with this line of questioning, but he stopped abruptly. *He needs to show that he didn't see Martin between eleven and twelve that night,* she thought. *This witness's testimony still hurts us.* "He needs to do more," she whispered to Chuck, but Christyson was on to his final point. He wanted to suggest that Winters could be wrong about the date.

"By the way, are there any time cards or written records that show Martin worked at the club on November 14, 1987?"

"No, we don't. I just paid him a percentage of what I earned."

Christyson sat down. Marie shook her head as she made eye contact with Chuck. She felt the momentum shifting toward the defendant for the first time that day.

The next witness was the defendant's sister, Carla Martin. Christyson objected as soon as the witness walked toward the witness chair.

"Your Honor, this witness has been sitting in the back of the courtroom all morning listening to Mrs. Grossman and the two police officers. You issued an order requiring the separation of witnesses. She's heard their testimony, and she can't unhear it. The law mandates a separation of witnesses for good reasons. Without it, witnesses can change their testimony to conform to what they've heard others say. I move that this witness be forbidden to testify. The defense has blatantly violated your order."

"Mr. Gauntner, how do you respond?"

"Your Honor, I had never met this witness before today. I didn't know she was in the back of the courtroom until the lunch recess when she came up to talk to her brother. I don't try cases by looking behind me. I told her to wait out in the hall when Mr. Winter testified this afternoon. I'm sorry this has happened, but it is an unforeseen and unintended mistake. I apologize to the court, but ask that the court exercise its discretion and allow Ms. Martin to testify."

"Mr. Gauntner, each side is responsible for policing its own witnesses. That was your job and nobody else's. However, I want your client to get a fair trial and not be deprived of any witnesses, particularly an alibi witness. I am going to exercise my discretion and allow Ms. Martin to testify, but I don't want this to happen again. Understood?"

"Yes, thank you, Your Honor."

Marie was miffed. The law had rules, and they were supposed to be followed. Why should she and the state be penalized because Mr. Gauntner couldn't control his own witnesses? This ruling just wasn't fair. The sinking feeling that had started with the first alibi witness grew stronger, and her jaw and head began to ache.

Carla Martin was eighteen, a year younger than her brother. She was attractive and conservatively dressed in a white blouse and a long dark skirt. As she began to talk, it was evident, however, that she was chewing gum. She was employed at Ray's Food, where she took orders and incoming calls. Directing the witness to November 14, Gauntner asked if she had seen her brother that day.

"He came to the house from work, him and Charles Winter. They were ready to go to a party at the Togo Club. and they came in. My brother got dressed. and they left to go to this party at around 11:30."

Christyson smiled as he jotted down some questions on his yellow pad. The sister's testimony conflicted directly with Winter's claim that he and Martin arrived at the Togo at 9:30 p.m. She also claimed that her brother had changed clothes before leaving with Winter. She was implying that they were going to a party there, not to work at the club. Hadn't Gauntner talked to this witness before he put her on the stand? *This witness is manna from heaven*, Christyson thought.

Marie grew excited as she listened to the sister. She had never tried a case before, but she longed to cross-examine this witness.

Gauntner realized that this witness was destroying the alibi for November 14 and immediately asked her about her brother's whereabouts on December 11.

"Well, on that day Chris came home around 5:30. He came into my room, where my infant son was. We both had company, and we sat in my room watching TV. Another of his friends came a little later to get him, but Chris wanted to take a shower. I'd say Chris left around ten after seven."

Gauntner asked no further questions of her.

The prosecutor zeroed in on her claim that her brother and Winter left for the Togo Club at 11:30. "Ms. Martin, if I were to tell you that Mr. Winter already testified that they arrived at the bar at 9:30, would he be right or would you be right?"

"That's what I said. They came to my house at 11:30 for Chris to change his clothes and they left."

"Are you saying that they were there twice?"

"Not really, but I know my brother was there earlier." Carla Martin began to fidget in the witness chair, and she looked at Gauntner, hoping he could protect her, but he looked away.

"Were they there once or twice that day?"

"All I can say is that they came back at 11:30."

"Would Mr. Winter be lying if he said that they were working at the Togo from 9:30 until 3 a.m. that night?"

"They could have gone to work and come back here and gone out again. Did you ask Mr. Winter that?" Carla Martin snapped.

"Please answer my question," the prosecutor countered.

"Did you ask him that question? That's what I want to know," Ms. Martin shot back.

"You're not asking the questions; I'm asking the questions."

"You ask him that question first, and then I will answer your question," the witness said angrily.

Judge Character intervened. "Miss Martin, you cannot debate with the attorney. You can only answer his questions. You can't ask him questions."

For the first time, Joe Grossman whispered to his mother. "This is great," he said, quickly returning his focus to the drama unfolding in front of him.

Christyson toyed with the idea of stopping his cross-examination right then and there, but he had not asked her about her brother's alleged whereabouts on December 11. When Christyson confronted her with the contradictions between her testimony and that of Thompson, she again got belligerent.

Changing his voice to a friendly, gentler tone, Christyson asked, "Ms. Martin, do you get along well with your brother?"

"Pretty much."

"And you would do anything for your brother, wouldn't you?"

"No."

"Are you saying that you would not?" Christyson said, feigning surprise.

"That's exactly what I'm saying," she said, irritation again showing in her voice. "He wouldn't do it for me when I was in trouble."

Marie and Chuck exchanged glances. "Did she say what I think she just said?" Chuck whispered.

"I think she just implied that her brother wouldn't lie for her when she was in legal trouble after she'd asked him to," Marie replied.

Christyson finished with the witness, and Gauntner chose not to question her again, certain that he could not rehabilitate her.

As Carla Martin rushed out of the courtroom, Joe Grossman flashed his mother a thumbs-up sign.

"We can't gloat," Marie whispered to him, but Joe continued to smile.

For his final alibi witness, Gauntner called Juanita Martin, the mother of Christopher Martin and the fiery Carla. After the sister's disastrous performance, Gauntner wondered whether there was any value in asking another family member to try to establish an alibi. Nevertheless, he dutifully questioned her, and she claimed that on December 11, 1987, her son had been in her apartment all day.

"We had a full house that day. I have a big, five-bedroom apartment, and three of my children was there with their friends, all spread out. A lot of comings and goings. Some of my friends were there too."

She said that Christopher had injured his foot a few days before and either hopped around the house or used a cane.

"I was fussing at him to get his prescription filled for that and to buy me a lottery ticket at the Pick and Pay."

She testified that Richard Thompson had arrived around 7:10.

"I know it was 7:10 because I was still arguing with him to get me that lottery ticket and the machines shut off at 7:15, and he told me that he didn't have time to do it now. They left in Richard's car, and then later that evening somebody came running into the house and told me they'd been arrested."

If Carla Martin had not testified first, the mother's story would have been difficult to disregard. She seemed credible, and if additional non-family guests had come forward to corroborate it, the alibi would have created doubt—perhaps reasonable doubt—about her son's whereabouts that evening.

For his cross-examination, Christyson chose to ask just a few questions. He was gambling that after his cross-examination of Carla Martin, the judge would find the "family alibi" untrustworthy.

"Did your son own a red Camaro with temporary tags?"

"Yes, he'd owned it for a couple of months, but it didn't work at the time."

"Can you explain why his inoperable Camaro was found at the Burger King parking lot that evening?"

If the prosecutor had expected to surprise the witness with that question, he did not. "It had been there for days," she replied evenly.

Christyson decided not to fence with her any longer. To his disappointment, she seemed to have an answer for everything and was not easily rattled. This realization was not lost on any of the Grossmans, who collectively sensed that the momentum had shifted again, this time in the wrong direction. Vested in the trial's outcome, they were overreacting to any development, good or bad.

Gauntner had decided not to put his client on the stand. He would test the sufficiency of the prosecution's evidence against his alibi witnesses. "We have no further witnesses, Your Honor. The defense rests," Gauntner told the judge.

Both attorneys suspected that the judge had already made up his mind, so they'd keep their closing arguments short. Because he had the burden of proof, the assistant prosecutor knew he would talk twice. He planned to provide opening comments, listen to the defense attorney's closing argument, and then speak again with his rebuttal argument.

"Your Honor, we have three crimes on three dates with strikingly similar details.

"Let's start with October 24, 1987. Brittany Kirkpatrick stops to place an order at a menu board. A man walks up to her driver's-side window and sticks a gun at her head. He forces his way into the back-seat, and another man gets into the front passenger seat. They ask her for an 'asset card'—not a bank card, but an 'asset card.' She doesn't have one. She gives them her purse. They drive around and eventually dump her in the middle of Hough late at night and drive off with her car. She is scared beyond belief, but she is one hundred percent sure that Christopher Martin is one of the two men.

"Let's move to November 14, 1987. Same thing. Carol Thornton stops to place an order at another fast-food restaurant. A man walks up to her open window, shoves a gun at her head, and tells her to move over. She does, and another man gets in the backseat behind her. What do they want? An 'asset card.' She realizes that any bank card will do and drives to an ATM, where she withdraws three hundred dollars at gunpoint and gives it to them. They drive off in her car, leaving her in the middle of nowhere. Who does she identify as the man who pulled the gun on her and drove her car? Christopher Martin."

Judge Character's face was unreadable as he listened to Christyson. In the audience, Joe Grossman hung on every word, while his parents were buoyed by the prosecutor's quick and efficient clip. He was like a marksman hitting every target.

"Then we come to December 11, 1987. It was to be exactly like the other two, but something went wrong. This time Richard Thompson had the gun and approached the car driven by Marie Grossman. Martin had given him the gun, told him what to say, and watched. Maybe he sent Thompson because he'd hurt his foot like his mother claimed, but this was still his crime. He'd set it in motion."

Marie nodded in agreement. She liked the way the prosecutor had taken some potentially damaging testimony and used it in his favor.

"When she offers him her purse, Thompson doesn't take it. He lets it drop. She senses that there is another man involved because he keeps looking over the car roof. He still wants her to drive them to an ATM, but she has no way of knowing this. He tries to force his way into the car. She thinks he's going to rape her. She hits the accelerator, and he shoots her with Martin's gun. I repeat—with Martin's gun, with Martin watching. She can't identify Martin, but his accomplice does. Who is in a better position to know whether Martin was part of this robbery? His partner, Richard Thompson.

"What's Martin's defense? Of course, he wasn't there at any of these robberies. Everybody has made a mistake in their identifications. He has alibi witnesses. Of course, he has alibi witnesses. He has alibi witnesses for November fourteenth and December eleventh, but where's his alibi witness for October twenty-fourth, when he's sticking a gun in Brittany Kirkpatrick's neck? He has no alibi witness for that robbery. And doesn't it strike you as strange that he claims that he wasn't anywhere near the Burger King when Marie Grossman was shot, yet his car was there in the parking lot when the police arrived?"

Marie grabbed Chuck's hand and squeezed it. She could hear the suppressed anger in the prosecutor's voice.

"Let's look at his alibi for November fourteenth. He's working at the Togo Club according to Charles Winter and Carla Martin. Wait a minute. In this courtroom, they give widely inconsistent accounts about that night. Carla says they left her house at 11:30. Charles says they arrived at the Club at 9:30. Which is it? Then Charles is working inside and Martin is working outside, and they don't see each other except for a few times that night, gaps of at least an hour, probably more. It's not like Martin and Winter are working side by side. There's plenty of time for Martin to sneak away and commit this crime.

"As for December eleventh, the defendant's mother and sister again tell different stories. Of course, they want to help the defendant, and I won't say more—other than their accounts are not credible.

"The state has provided testimony that positively identifies Martin as the perpetrator each time this has happened—in October, November, and December. We've demonstrated beyond a reasonable doubt that Christopher Martin committed these crimes. The state would ask that he be found guilty on all eight counts."

As he concluded his remarks, Christyson turned from the center podium and stared at Christopher Martin, who shook his head at him in response.

Timothy Gauntner stood and walked gravely to the podium.

"Your Honor, I do not have to remind you of the state's obligation in this case. Proof beyond a reasonable doubt means just that. It does not mean a case built on supposition, guesswork, shortcuts, and perjured testimony. I, too, will comment on the evidence, one incident at a time.

"We begin with Brittany Kirkpatrick, a sweet young woman who tells us a frightening story. I was moved by her account, as I'm sure you were too. However, before we blame Christopher Martin for that crime, we need to be sure that he actually did it. The law requires nothing short of this.

"The only thing that is clear from Ms. Kirkpatrick's testimony is that she was terrified by what happened to her that night. It is that terror that makes her testimony unreliable. Because of her fright, she has very minimal recall of the actual details.

"I am not talking about minor details but major ones. She cannot remember which of the two men pointed the gun at her. That's a huge hole in her memory. She doesn't know where the two men sat in her car. Was my client right next to her or was he behind her? What does that tell you about the accuracy of her memory?

"On direct exam, the prosecutor asked Ms. Kirkpatrick to describe the other man in the car. She said that my client's accomplice was smaller than he was. That's interesting. Richard Thompson is six inches taller than Christopher Martin. The prosecutor has told you that this same duo committed three fast-food robberies. The prosecutor charged Richard Thompson with the robbery involving Ms. Kirkpatrick too. The prosecutor says Thompson was there on October twenty-fourth. That means one thing—Ms. Kirkpatrick's description of him is incredibly off. If she can't describe Thompson at all, what does that say about her identification of my client? She's wrong there too."

Marie had a sinking feeling in her stomach. She'd expected Gauntner to give a half-hearted or disjointed closing argument, but he was making solid points. She, too, was beginning to doubt Kirkpatrick's identification. If she had uncertainty, what was the judge thinking?

Gauntner continued, "There is another thing to consider here. When the prosecutor put Richard Thompson on the stand, why didn't he ask him if Christopher Martin was at the Kirkpatrick robbery scene? The prosecutor asks you to believe all of Richard Thompson's testimony—all of it. When I asked Thompson if he was at the Kirkpatrick robbery, he denied he was there. If they are such an inseparable pair, then that means my client wasn't there either. The prosecutor can't have it both ways.

"As I said, I feel very badly for Ms. Kirkpatrick. However, convicting the wrong man for her ordeal does nothing to undo the wrongs committed against her. It only multiplies the injustice. The law, and in particular reasonable doubt, doesn't allow you to put a man in prison with such a lack of proof."

The judge's expression remained impassive. *Is he agreeing with Gauntner?* Marie asked herself.

"Let's move on to the robbery of Carol Thornton." Gauntner's voice seemed stronger, and there was a tinge of indignation in it. "Ms. Thornton testified that she was with her assailants for up to an hour and a half. They drove around, unsure where to go, making wrong turns, and arguing where to drop her off.

"That testimony does not fit with that of Charles Winter. Mr. Winter is a hardworking man who has made it his mission to find work for young people like my client. Christopher Martin worked with him at a club that evening from 9:30 p.m. to 3 a.m. Mr. Winter testified that he saw my client at least once an hour that entire evening.

"Again, if the prosecutor wanted to show that my client was at the Thornton robbery, he simply had to ask his star witness, Richard Thompson, if my client was there. Thompson was charged with that robbery. He never asked him that question.

"Ms. Thornton's identification is faulty too. She admitted that this evening was 'worse than a nightmare.' Those were her words, not mine. She, too, was so frightened that she was unable to properly identify her assailant. She couldn't identify Richard Thompson as being at the robbery. If she couldn't identify Thompson after being in the car with him for an hour and a half, how could she possibly identify her other assailant with any certainty? She can't. Her identification is not to be trusted.

"Finally, we get to Mrs. Grossman and December 11, 1987. Mrs. Grossman never saw my client at the scene—not at any time. She saw one person at the scene and that person was Richard Thompson.

"Richard Thompson acted alone that evening. He worked out a deal with the prosecutor to get six charges dropped against him. In return, he had to implicate my client in the Grossman incident. He did so to save his own skin, and he can't be believed.

"Christopher Martin was at home with his family when Thompson committed this crime by himself. My client was limping and using a cane and could not have been able to move quickly to assist in any robbery that night. No one has disputed this fact.

"Your Honor, there has been a total failure of proof on all three crimes and all eight counts. We would ask that you find the defendant not guilty on all charges. Thank you."

The prosecutor shot from his chair for his rebuttal. "I'll be brief. Brittany Kirkpatrick was one hundred percent certain that Christopher Martin was one of the men who robbed her and stole her car. Carol Thornton was positive that Christopher Martin was one of the two men who robbed her. These are not difficult identifications. Martin was not wearing a mask or anything to disguise his appearance. Richard Thompson was in a unique position to know whether Martin was involved in the Grossman crime. None of these witnesses is confused. None of them hesitated. Each of them is positive that Martin participated in these heinous crimes.

"I won't rehash the inconsistent stories told by the alibi witnesses. Mrs. Martin admitted that her son owned a red Camaro, the same Camaro that was parked in the Burger King lot prior to and after the robbery attempt on Marie Grossman.

"There is no doubt that Christopher Martin is guilty on all eight counts as charged. Thank you."

Christyson returned to his seat and began gathering up his papers.

"What's going to happen now?" Joe Grossman whispered to his mother.

"I'm not sure, but usually the judge takes a few days to sift through the evidence and then announces the decision in open court," she replied.

Judge Character cleared his throat and said, "The court has heard all the evidence in this case and will find as follows: that Christopher Martin is guilty on all counts as charged."

Both Christyson and Gauntner appeared stunned by the judge's speedy decision. Looking at Gauntner, the judge said, "Counsel, would you and your client approach the bench, please?"

The defense attorney and his client made their way to the front of the court.

"I am going to defer sentencing until the probation department has prepared a presentencing report. Sentencing will take place on June twenty-seventh at 10 a.m. The defendant is to be remanded to the custody of the Cuyahoga County sheriff pending sentence. Anything else?"

"Nothing else, Judge," Gauntner answered.

Marie, Chuck, and Joe walked over to the prosecutor to congratulate and thank him.

"I am very grateful," Marie said. "I had my doubts about the process, but you made it work for me and the other women. On behalf of all of us, thank you."

"You're welcome. This was an important case for us. We've wanted to get both of these guys off the streets for a long time. I think Martin was the really bad one here," Christyson said, still concerned that Marie didn't approve of the deal that he'd struck with Thompson.

"I'll be attending the sentencing," Marie said.

"If you want to speak at the sentencing, you're allowed to. It's up to you. On the other hand, you can call me and I will incorporate your thoughts into my presentation. Just let me know."

"I'll let you know," Marie said. "Thanks again."

As they walked out of the courtroom, Marie tried to understand her feelings. She alternated between feeling energized and then disappointed. For the foreseeable future, she was safe from these men. That should have been reason to celebrate, but she could not. Deep inside, she knew that something terribly important had been taken from her. Whatever that was, the criminal justice system would never return it to her. She understood that healing, if that was possible, would be something that she'd have to work out on her own.

10

THE SENTENCING

The mood in Courtroom 17A was subdued and somber, somewhat like a church sanctuary before a service begins. There were those who gossiped quietly about events in their lives and others who sat in silence, overwhelmed by their own personal problems. Judge Character had scheduled several sentencings this morning, and most of the courtroom was filled with the family and friends of the criminal defendants about to learn their fate. Marie, Joe, and Chuck tried to avoid the defendants' family members and slipped into the second row among several lawyers and other court personnel.

Marie was tense, concerned that Judge Character might mete out light sentences or that family members might wail and scream if the sentences were harsher than what they'd expected. There was also the prospect of making eye contact with Thompson and Martin again. The combination made her stomach churn. In contrast, Chuck and Joe sat calmly. They were there to support Marie and to satisfy their own curiosity about this last step in the criminal justice system.

After a few minutes, Robert Christyson sat down at a trial table directly in front of them. Taking a folder from his briefcase, he turned and nodded to Marie and her family. Two defense attorneys, Timothy Gauntner and a woman Marie had never seen before, whispered near the other table, their expressions unconcerned.

The courtroom took on an air of expectancy when the bailiff materialized almost magically and slipped into his chair behind the witness box. He'd entered from a private door, not visible from the gallery, but located behind the tall wood-paneled wall that served as the backdrop to the judge's bench. The bailiff picked up a phone from his desk, and a few minutes later, two sheriff's deputies escorted Christopher Martin and Richard Thompson into the courtroom.

Marie assumed that Thompson would be sentenced first because he was taken directly to the trial table. The woman attorney sat next to him, while Gauntner leaned against a nearby wall. Thompson sat hunched at the table, his hands folded in his lap and his head bowed, almost as if he were praying. In contrast, Martin sat upright in the front row, surveyed the courtroom, and glowered.

For the next five minutes, the bailiff read the morning paper and periodically looked over his shoulder. When he saw the judge behind the front panel, he nodded to him, stood up, and called the court into session.

After taking the bench, Judge Character began, "We are here on Case Number CR297456A, involving Richard Thompson. Mr. Thompson was charged in an eight-count indictment. Last month he pled guilty to two counts, aggravated robbery and felonious assault. In exchange for that plea, counts three through eight were dropped. Mr. Thompson, has your attorney explained that each of the remaining two counts carries a gun specification? That means there is a three-year mandatory prison time for those crimes because you used a gun. Do you understand that?"

The woman attorney stood and said that she had explained that to her client. Thompson nodded.

"Very well then. Counsel, have you read the presentence report prepared by the probation department?"

"Yes, Your Honor."

"Anything from the prosecutor?"

"No, Your Honor."

Turning to Thompson's attorney, the judge asked, "Do you have anything to say on your client's behalf?"

"Mr. Thompson understands the gravity of what he has done. Ever since he was arrested, he has cooperated with the police. He agreed to testify against Christopher Martin, and his testimony helped convict the codefendant. Mr. Thompson is nineteen years old and has no prior criminal record. I would ask that he be sentenced to a minimum term.

"Thank you."

"Mr. Thompson, do you have anything to say before I pass sentence upon you?"

Standing with his hands in his pockets, Thompson spoke in a quiet voice. "I just want to say that I am sorry for what I done. I didn't mean to shoot Mrs. Grossman. That was an accident when her car moved away from me. I'm sorry she got hurt."

Rubbing his moustache, the judge looked down at Thompson and cleared his throat. "It is the decision of this court that you will be sentenced to the Ohio State Reformatory in Mansfield, Ohio, under both counts. On count one, you will serve a term of five to twenty-five years, and on count two, a term of three to fifteen years. These sentences will run concurrently. This means that the two terms will run together. You will serve between five and twenty-five years in prison. Do you understand?"

Thompson nodded.

Christyson rose for the first time. "I don't know if this needs to be on the record, but we ask that Mr. Thompson be kept apart from Mr. Martin in the jail until he is transferred to the Ohio State Reformatory."

"Yes, the defendant will be housed in a separate part of the jail from Mr. Martin until such time that he goes to the Ohio State Reformatory."

As soon as Thompson turned away from the judge, a sheriff's deputy met him and began to escort him out of the courtroom. Hearing a woman gasp and stifle a cry, Marie turned and looked behind her. A middle-aged, heavyset black woman held a white handkerchief to her face while a man, seated next to her, put his arm around her. In that same row, a teenage girl sat with an infant in her arms. She, too, was crying, unable to watch as Thompson marched past them.

Returning her gaze to the front of the courtroom, Marie saw that Christopher Martin and Gauntner were now standing in front of the judge, who was again explaining the charges and the various gun specifications. "Mr. Gauntner, do you have anything to say before the court imposes its sentence upon Mr. Martin?"

"Thank you, Your Honor. Mr. Martin has denied his involvement in this matter. I understand that his case did come before you and you found him guilty. I would request that this court consider his young age in any sentence that may be imposed."

"Anything else?"

Gauntner looked to his right and saw Marie and her family in the gallery. "Uh, yes, Your Honor. I would like the record to further indicate that it was the codefendant, Mr. Thompson, who shot the woman."

Judge Character looked at Christopher Martin. "Mr. Martin, do you have anything you would like to say?"

"Well, not really. I'm sorry for what happened to the lady. That's it."

Judge Character took off his glasses and stared at Martin. "That's it, Mr. Martin?"

"Yeah."

Shaking his head, Judge Character began, "I heard this case and all the evidence that was presented. Mr. Martin, what you and your companion did was reprehensible. What you did had an effect on the entire community. You brought shame and disrepute to the black community by your actions while legitimate neighborhood businesses feared that their customers were not safe. You and Mr. Thompson terrorized defenseless women. From the presentence report, I see that you were using marijuana and cocaine at the time of these crimes. The fact that you were on dope at the time just doesn't cut it with me. Neither the law nor the court finds that to be a legal excuse or mitigating factor for your behavior."

Chuck could hear the indignation in the judge's voice. Behind him, he heard a woman whisper to her companion, "But he didn't do any of that. He wasn't even there."

The judge continued. "You caused enormous psychological damage to one victim and, in one case, great physical damage."

Marie knew that the judge was speaking about Brittany Kirkpatrick and herself.

"You told the court that you were sorry. That is grossly and totally inadequate. You have not admitted any responsibility for these crimes, and I find that very troubling. I will impose your sentences with that in mind."

Judge Character then pronounced a sentence of ten to twenty-five years for each of the three robberies. Because each charge carried a gun specification of three years, Judge Character sentenced Martin to nine years of mandatory prison time. Unlike Thompson, he would serve his sentences consecutively, not concurrently. In the end, he would be in prison for thirty to seventy-five years.

"Can I ask one question, sir?" Martin asked. Despite calling the judge "sir," his tone was rebellious. "What do you mean by 'consecutive'?"

"That means that you will serve one sentence of ten years, and after you have completed serving that sentence, you will start serving the second term of ten years. After you complete the second sentence, you'll start serving the third period of ten years."

Martin had never expected the judge to impose such a harsh sentence and could no longer hide his anger. He shot back, "I watched this case on TV where the guy did—"

The judge interrupted him. "I don't care what you watched on television. That's entertainment. This is real life."

"I didn't do nothing. I got an unfair trial. Everything was based on circumstantial evidence."

"I listened to the testimony, and it was direct evidence, Mr. Martin."

"I don't know if you listened to anything or not," Martin said. If the judge was going to send him away for decades, he was going to say his piece.

"Mr. Martin, you will have an opportunity to appeal my verdict. Because you are indigent, we will take steps to have someone file an appeal for you. That will be all," the judge said, his voice impatient and stern.

"Wait. I got more to say. Richard Thompson did these crimes, not me."

"That will be enough, Mr. Martin."

Struck by a new thought and oblivious to his prior belligerence, Martin blurted, "Am I eligible for shock parole or anything like that?"

"No, sir," the judge replied, suppressing a smile.

"I've got to do the mandatory, even though I didn't do nothing?"

The judge ignored him. "Court costs will be attached. Mr. Gauntner, will you see to it that a notice of appeal is perfected and that either your office or the Public Defender Office is appointed to represent Mr. Martin?"

Nodding solemnly, Gauntner said, "Yes, Your Honor. I will contact the Public Defender Office and take steps to see that it perfects the appeal." He was anxious to pass responsibility to another attorney.

In the back of the courtroom, Marie heard two women talking, their voices loud and emotional.

"If your son hadn't testified against Christopher, he wouldn't be doing so much time," one said. "What he did to save himself, well, it makes me sick. How many times was that boy at my house, eating my food and enjoying our company? And that's how he repays us."

The other woman appeared to hold her ground. "Well, it was your son who got Richard hooked on drugs. Your son came up with this scheme and talked Richard into it."

Joe tapped his mother on the elbow and said, "Remember, you said you'd ask Mr. Christyson for me."

Marie remembered that at Joe's high school, the students were allowed to shadow someone in the workplace for two days. Joe had asked if he could follow Robert Christyson.

"Sure, let's go up and ask him, but why don't you ask him yourself?" she said.

After Joe explained the shadow experience to Christyson, the assistant prosecutor said, "Oh sure, I've done that a couple of times already. Just give me a call when you have the dates. There's a lot going on at the prosecutor's office, and I'm sure we can keep things interesting for you."

Immediately after the hearing, Marie had intended to ask Christyson some general and specific questions about parole. She knew that convicted felons could seek parole before their sentences were completed, and she wanted to know exactly when these defendants would first be eligible. However, Joe's inquiry had caused her to momentarily forget her question. As she stood there with Christyson, she struggled to remember it.

"There was a question I meant to ask you, but I can't remember it right now," she said, shrugging her shoulders. "Well, thank you very much for all your hard work. I'm very satisfied with your result."

When she and her family stepped into the elevator a few minutes later, she remembered her question. She considered returning to the courtroom to ask it but decided to call him later. She didn't have to know right then and there when either defendant would be eligible for parole. Neither of these men would be a threat to her for many years, and she felt safe with that knowledge.

As they descended in the elevator, Marie thought about the other legal matter that was on her mind. After she'd learned that Thompson and Martin had terrorized Brittany Kirkpatrick almost two months before her at the same Burger King, she'd been very upset with the restaurant and its failure to improve security after the first incident. She'd contacted an attorney to discuss whether Burger King bore some responsibility for what had happened to her. He'd said he didn't know but had contacted Christyson and requested the police investigation. Christyson explained that he couldn't release any of the investigation until the criminal case had been completed. Now that the two assailants were on their way to prison, Marie would ask the prosecutor to send her attorney the police file.

When she got home, she left a message with Christyson's secretary. "Please let him know that I have two things that I want to talk to him about. First, I want to know when these defendants will be eligible for parole. Second, I am also wondering if he can send his file to the attorney who contacted him on my behalf."

"I'll give him the message," the secretary replied.

Part II

Forcing Change

11

THE CALL

I was both surprised and curious when my secretary told me that Marie Grossman was on the other line. Two months earlier in mid-December, my wife, Leslee, had visited her in the hospital and then briefed me on the unprovoked shooting that could have killed her friend. I guessed that Marie might be calling to get some answers about the criminal case involving her assailants. But if she had questions about that, I couldn't help her. In the nine years I'd been a lawyer, I'd never handled anything in the criminal arena. Instead, my practice had been limited to civil injury cases in the local courts.

When I picked up the receiver, I wasn't sure how to begin, and I paused for a moment before finally speaking. "Hello Marie," I said. "I still can't believe this happened to you. How are you feeling?"

"I'm doing better," came the response from the other end.

For the next few minutes, she told me about her recovery and how lucky she felt to be alive. She apologized for her speech, which was slow and deliberate, but I told her that I had no trouble understanding her.

After a pause, she said, "I'd like to explore whether Burger King could be legally responsible for what happened to me. I know you do personal injury work, and I wanted to get your thoughts."

It was not unusual for friends and acquaintances to call me after they'd been injured. Whether the case had merit or not, I listened to their story, explained the law, and told them whether they had a claim worth pursuing. When I told them that they didn't, some would argue with me, but most would thank me for my advice, often embarrassed that they'd troubled me.

I was always surprised by the number of people who thought that business owners were liable for any injuries occurring on their property regardless of the circumstances. However, this just wasn't the law. Businesses only needed to take reasonable steps to eliminate dangers that they knew about or should have known about.

As this thought flashed through my mind, I asked, "Why do you think Burger King might be responsible for the shooting?" Truth be told, I suspected that she'd probably been a victim of a random criminal act that the restaurant could neither have predicted nor protected her against.

"Well, these same two men robbed and abducted another woman at that same Burger King about two months before my incident. I don't think the restaurant took any steps to make the drive-thru safer," she said. "It's as if they didn't care."

"Are you sure of this?" I asked. My initial skepticism vanished, and she had my full attention.

"I found out about this prior incident a few months ago," she said. "I was at the preliminary hearing when the investigating detective testified about it. I was dumbfounded by the information then, and it's still troubling me now."

Without further investigation, I couldn't tell if she had a claim. All I knew was that these facts were disturbing, and that alone was enough to seek more information. I would be cautious for now. There were usually two sides to a story, and at this point, we had very limited facts.

"Marie, if you'd like us to help you, we'll do whatever we can. I can't say if there's a case or not, but I have a feeling that this will bother you until you have some answers."

"I do have one immediate question that I hope you can answer," she said. "Have you ever worked on a case like this before—you know, where a business was held responsible because it didn't take measures to protect a customer against a criminal attack?"

"Actually, we just resolved a case like this a few months ago," I said and then told her a little about it. The firm, through my older brother, Jim, had represented a man who'd been shot in a bar parking lot after a fight erupted between motorcycle gang members. Our client had not been part of the melee but simply had been in the wrong place at the wrong time. Because the bar's parking lot had been the site of frequent fights, we argued that the bar should have hired a security guard to protect its patrons. We'd employed a security expert who had reviewed the case and reached the same conclusion.

"That's good. I'm glad your firm has some experience with this," she said. "I'd really like to talk to you about this in more detail."

"Sure," I replied. "I doubt that you're in much condition to drive to my office. Do you want me to stop by your house sometime next week?"

"I'd like that. I do have questions, and I'm really not sure what to do or if I even want to do anything. I should tell you that Chuck is very much against personal injury lawsuits."

"Oh," I said, thrown off by her last comment. "Do you mean he's against all injury cases or just this one?"

She then explained that Chuck's company made fire-retardant clothing for firemen, steel workers, and other laborers and, at one time, had manufactured it with asbestos. As a result, his company had been sued in hundreds of asbestos lawsuits, many in which the litigants couldn't prove that they had ever used his products. His company's liability insurance had been exhausted, and these ongoing lawsuits could eventually bankrupt the business.

"He has a very negative opinion about the civil justice system and injury lawsuits. I thought I should warn you in case he's at home when you stop by," she said.

Because she'd reached out to me, I realized that, at the very least, she wanted to talk about the legal issues. "Well, I can appreciate his feeling," I said. "We can get together and talk, and you can decide later what you want to do."

If she ultimately decided that she didn't want to pursue her claim, I would understand. Lawsuits, particularly civil cases involving serious injuries, often required clients to spend enormous amounts of emotional capital. Litigation could fill their lives with stress, disappointment, and confusion. For some individuals, it was healthier to simply move on with their lives rather than experience several years of legal conflict and personal turmoil. Marie was a friend first. I could outline her options, and she could decide.

We decided to meet in three days, and I told her that I would bring my partner, Ben Barrett, with me if he was available.

After I hung up, I walked down the hall to talk to Ben Barrett, who at age forty-eight was the firm's senior partner. He'd taken on that role two and a half years earlier, after my sixty-five-year-old father, the firm's founder, had died of cancer. We limited our practice to civil litigation and, in the vast majority of our cases, represented injured people in their claims against insurance companies.

After my father's death, Ben and I had teamed up on many of our more important cases. I continued to handle small and medium-sized cases on my own, but on larger cases, I helped him with the investigation and groundwork leading up to trial, and then Ben tried the case. It was a great way for me to observe and learn. Over the past nine years, I'd watched him try many cases, and I marveled at his skill in the courtroom. He was persuasive, strategic, and quick. To the jury, he evinced sincerity and common sense and bonded with them easily. Beyond his trial skills, I valued his judgment and legal mind.

Sitting behind his large desk, Ben was reviewing a deposition transcript. I took a chair across from him and asked if I could interrupt. He put down the deposition and looked at me expectantly.

I explained what I knew about Marie's potential case. When I told him about the prior incident, he nodded and said, "That's unbelievable. The same two guys."

He wanted to know more about Marie. I told him that she was an attorney, and her husband owned his own company. They had two children and lived in Lakewood.

"Where is this restaurant—what did you say, Euclid and East Eighty-Eighth?" Ben asked.

"East Eighty-Fifth," I said, correcting him.

"When I was an insurance adjuster and ventured into that neighborhood, I was always looking over my shoulder. It's a tough area with a lot of crime. Most jurors will know that, and some may actually think it's more violent than it really is. In the end, I don't know what a jury will do. They could side with the business owner and conclude that it's almost impossible to keep a parking lot safe from an isolated robbery."

"I think it's worth investigating," I offered.

"So do I," Ben said. "I'm just trying to look at this from the other side." He checked his schedule and told me he could join me on Friday.

☆ ☆ ☆

It was drizzling when Ben and I parked in Marie's driveway on Lake Road in Lakewood that Friday in early March. She met us at the side door that opened from the driveway into an enclosed porch that she had turned into her home office. She was dressed in jeans and a bulky gray sweater and led us into her living room. She must have been sleeping on the couch because a pillow and folded blanket were on one end. Her cheeks were swollen, almost as if she had the mumps. The entrance wound on her left cheek was purple and puffy, about the size of a nickel. On the other side, the bullet had blown away skin and tissue in the shape of the letter C, and this exit wound was slightly smaller than its counterpart.

After introducing Ben, I asked her to tell him what had happened on December 11. Ben and I listened intently, absorbed by her description of that harrowing night. Not only could she tell us what had happened, but she could remember her actual thoughts during the encounter. We had heard hundreds of clients tell their stories, but none like Marie. Her vivid details seemed to transport us into her car as the events unfolded.

After we finished talking about her injuries and prognosis, she wanted to know a little about Ben. She knew me, but Marie was the type of individual who was interested in knowing other people's stories.

"Do you want the long story or the short one?" he asked.

"Give me the long story. If I get bored, I'll let you know," Marie said.

"I grew up in Salem, Ohio. My dad was the high school football coach. As a freshman, I secretly tried out for the freshman football team, but I was a scrawny kid, not more than ninety pounds then. My dad found out about it later that day, and although he did not forbid me to play on the freshman squad, he made a phone call, and we drove over to another teacher's house, where I met the advisor to the high school debate team. I quit football and joined the debate team, and that's when the idea of becoming a lawyer first surfaced. I went to John Carroll for my undergraduate degree, got married while in college, took a job with Travelers Insurance, and eventually went to night law school at Cleveland State. Are you bored yet?" Ben asked.

"No, please go on. I said I'd tell you," Marie said.

"I had a job lined up with an insurance defense firm, but at the last minute, I got an offer from a plaintiff's personal injury firm headed by

Mike Shane. I accepted Mike's offer and tried a lot of cases for Mike. He invariably gave me the 'dogs'—you know, the cases that he shouldn't have accepted in the first place. Early on, I was getting beat up pretty regularly and soundly. While driving home one afternoon after a day in trial, I saw some ditch diggers along the side of the road and thought they had a better job than I did. But with each case, I improved. I was trying one of Mike's cases against David's father, Ray, around 1969. Ray had won this case when Mike had tried it, but it had been reversed on appeal and was to be tried again. This time Mike sent me in his place, and I won the case against Ray."

"Oh, you did. That's interesting," Marie said. After my father had died, she'd come to the funeral and learned a few things about him, particularly his reputation as a top-notch trial lawyer.

"Well, I got a little assist from the judge," Ben said with a laugh. "The judge had been the prosecutor in a celebrated murder trial— maybe five years earlier—and Ray had won an acquittal for the defendant in that case. During my trial, it was clear that the judge was still upset about the murder verdict. He ruled against Ray in every conceivable way."

Marie looked at me and raised her eyebrows.

"A few months later, Ray asked me if I would be interested in coming out to Lorain County to practice with him. I said yes, and I've been here since 1970. I've tried dozens and dozens of cases—both for insurance companies and for injured people like you. I enjoy what I do and the challenges of trial work."

"I see," Marie replied. "Well, I've told you my story, and you've told me yours. Let's talk some more about Burger King."

We nodded.

Marie continued, "I'm just so angry that they didn't do anything to make the drive-thru more secure after this happened to the other woman. They could have added a security guard or a video camera or more lighting. I mean, they had six weeks to do something. I also wonder if they've made any changes since I've been shot. Could something similar happen to another woman?"

We didn't answer her rhetorical question but let her continue.

"I keep thinking that if I don't do something, they'll never make their restaurants safer. Sometimes it takes a lawsuit to force a corporation to make needed changes. What do you think?"

"Unfortunately, that can be true," Ben said. "We see it a lot. It's only when a company is hit with a large jury verdict that it finally focuses on the problem."

"I think that cases like yours are changing the way businesses address security issues," I added.

For decades, businesses had successfully blamed the criminal as the sole cause of an attack that occurred on their property. They'd argued that the criminal's unforeseeable and unpredictable crime was something that they couldn't reasonably have guarded against. That had all changed with one case, and I decided to tell Marie about it.

"There was another woman who took a strong stand against a business that had failed to protect her. Do you know who I'm talking about?" I asked.

"I guess I don't," Marie said.

"I'm talking about the singer Connie Francis. Does that ring a bell?" I asked.

"You know, I do remember something about that. I think they did a segment about her case on *60 Minutes*, but refresh my memory," Marie urged.

"Connie Francis had rented a two-bedroom suite on the second floor of a Howard Johnson motel near a music festival where she was performing. Unbeknownst to her, the sliding glass door on the balcony had a defective latch. In fact, the latches throughout the motel frequently failed to keep out burglars, and criminals had repeatedly broken into rooms. While the singer was in her room, an unknown assailant entered through the sliding glass doors and raped her."

Marie winced and looked away when I mentioned the rape. I continued, "She and her husband sued Howard Johnson in New Jersey state court, claiming that the motel was negligent because it knew about the problem and didn't replace or fix the doors. The defense argued that the criminal's act was the sole reason for her injuries, but the jurors didn't agree. They found that the crime was foreseeable and preventable and awarded her a large verdict.

"After that, apartment owners, shopping center owners, and other businesses were aware that they had to do more to protect their customers. And they began to make their properties more secure from criminal acts. So yes, cases like yours can bring about change," I said.

We were all silent for a few moments, and then Marie spoke. "I really do feel that I need to do something to make this less likely to happen to someone else, but I just don't know how Chuck would react to all of this," Marie said. "Did David tell you about the asbestos lawsuits?"

Ben nodded.

"I've been thinking about this and have an idea," Marie volunteered. "I'm not sure I want to proceed with a case at this point, but I'd like someone to investigate this while I make up my mind."

"We could do that," Ben said.

"I just need a couple of months to continue thinking about this and then, of course, Chuck and I need to talk this through," she said.

"Yeah, I think that's a good idea," Ben said. "You need someone to gather documents, take photographs of the scene, and obtain witness statements while memories are still fresh."

"We'll get started and report to you periodically," I said.

"Then just let us know what you ultimately decide," Ben said.

12

FIRST STEPS

Trying to investigate a case prior to filing the suit papers is like running a race with your legs hobbled—you can't get very far. Your opponent has no incentive to cooperate and divulge material that could be used against it. Because of this, we weren't going to contact the restaurant owners in hopes of obtaining useful information. That would have been futile.

I soon discovered that the prosecutor's office was not willing to provide us with any of its investigation now. I spoke with the assistant prosecutor, Robert Christyson, and, although he was cordial and sympathetic to Marie's plight, he was forbidden by internal rules to provide detailed police reports and witness statements to outsiders until the criminal cases were closed. He obviously wanted to keep his investigation close to the vest, something I could understand. Before I hung up, however, I exacted a promise that he would send the reports to me as soon the cases against Thompson and Martin were finished.

Although we weren't sure if Marie would ultimately go forward with her case, we proceeded with the mind-set that she would. For that reason, we didn't delay in gathering whatever evidence was available in the public domain.

Real estate records revealed that the restaurant in question was not owned by Burger King Corporation. Although Burger King owned many of its own restaurants, most, like this one, were franchised to local businesspeople. A businessman by the name of Harold Stillwater owned the franchise for this restaurant, and he, in turn, had assigned it to a company called Quick Eats Enterprises, Inc., which also operated a number of other Burger King restaurants in the Cleveland area.

If we proceeded with the case, we would want both Burger King Corporation and the local business entity as defendants in our case. The case would be more likely to cause change and improve security nation-wide if Burger King Corporation were a defendant. But how would we be able to make a case against Burger King if Burger King didn't actually operate the restaurant? We'd only know that after we'd filed a lawsuit and learned how much control Burger King exerted over its franchised restaurants.

Three days after our meeting with Marie, I was in a car headed for East Eighty-Fifth Street and Euclid to see firsthand the Burger King property. I was accompanied by Brad Clark, a college student at nearby Lorain County Community College whom we'd recently hired to file pleadings and perform other odd jobs on a part-time basis. We'd soon learned that Brad had a nose for investigating, and I often sent him to interview witnesses. Once, I'd even had him do surveillance on an op-posing party whom I'd suspected of exaggerating his injuries. He'd re-turned with video of the man lifting heavy logs at a worksite, something totally at odds with the man's supposedly chronic back condition.

This afternoon we set out to take photographs of the scene and to scout the property. The weather had warmed, and the streets, side-walks, and parking lots were shedding whatever snow still lingered on them. Around 1:30 p.m., we parked my car in the Cleveland Play House parking lot across the street from the Burger King. Unlike the open Burger King lot, the Cleveland Play House parking area was completely surrounded by a tall, elegant black wrought-iron fence. From this loca-tion, I pointed my Minolta's telephoto lens through a fence opening and snapped away at the Burger King.

We got back into the car and drove over to the Burger King.

"Let's order something from the drive-thru," Brad suggested.

Although we had already eaten lunch, we followed the same path as Marie through the lot, stopping at the menu board and rolling down the driver's window to place an order for a chocolate milkshake and a Coke.

As we waited for the employee to confirm our order, the menu board's speaker sputtered with static. We looked for a video camera but didn't see one mounted anywhere. After we picked up our order and drove by the front of the building, we peered into the restaurant, where a woman and her two small children sat at a table eating their food. The sun had poked through the clouds, and the restaurant's exterior sparkled from the light striking its wet surface. At this moment, the restaurant looked nondescript and safe—like hundreds of others found in secure neighborhoods across the country.

As if reading my mind, Brad said, "Doesn't seem dangerous, does it?"

"Not now, but based on what we know, I wouldn't want to be here after dark."

We parked my car in the back and got out. I put a regular lens on my camera and began taking photographs of the menu board, the building, and the back lot. Almost immediately, a young employee came out of the back door carrying broken-down cardboard boxes to throw into the dumpster.

"Hey, why are you taking photographs back here?" he asked as he approached us.

I hung the camera strap around my neck and allowed the camera to fall to my waist. I walked over to him and said, "We represent the woman who was shot here a couple of months ago. We're taking a few photographs as part of our investigation."

"You got permission to do that?" he asked.

"I can step over onto the sidewalk and take them from there if it bothers you," I told him.

He seemed to weigh my words for a moment. "No, that's okay. I was just wondering."

Brad asked, "Were you working the night she was shot?" His question surprised me and was improper. Attorneys are subject to various ethical rules, one of which forbids questioning a potential defendant's employees outside the presence of the defendant's attorney. Brad didn't know that.

"You don't need to answer that," I interjected.

The employee gave me a confused stare and then ignored me. "I wasn't working that night, but I've heard a lot about it."

I squeezed Brad's shoulder and whispered to him, "We're not allowed to talk to their employees at this stage."

He nodded, but I could tell he was disappointed that I'd cut him off before he'd found out more.

"We'll just be a few minutes more," I told the employee.

"What's your name?" he asked, his tone turning sharp for the first time.

I pulled out a business card from my wallet and handed it to him. He studied it for a moment and then stuffed it into his pants pocket.

"Never heard of you," he said as he tossed the cardboard into the dumpster.

We hadn't intended to do much else that afternoon, but because we were already in Cleveland, I decided to make one more stop, at the Cleveland city hall and its building department. After parking, we walked to the city hall, an impressive stone building that looked like it belonged in Washington, D.C., rather than downtown Cleveland. Its second-floor balcony with its imposing pillars seemed to be the perfect spot for a national leader to address a huge crowd. However, we were headed inside to a more prosaic setting, Room 501, where the city's building records were stored.

After introducing myself, I explained that we wanted all of the building records for a Burger King restaurant located at 8515 Euclid. When I told the employee, a man named Tony, that a woman had been shot there, he perked up.

"I'm particularly interested in obtaining a drawing of the building showing how it is laid out on the property plot. Also, if you have the records for any improvements to the building, we would like to see those too."

A few minutes later, Tony was back with a manila folder about three-quarters of an inch thick. I'd expected him to just hand it over and let me try to decipher it, but instead, he opened it and began explaining the documents one by one. Because Tony either was bored or was just naturally friendly, he seemed to relish telling us about the documents. The restaurant had been built in 1971 and the drive-thru added eight years later. There had been no additional changes since then. I thanked him and asked him to copy the file and send it to us.

"I'll have to charge you for the copies. Is that okay?" Tony asked. "I'll need the money today."

"Sure, that's fine," I said. I wrote him a check, and he gave me a receipt.

I really didn't think that any of the documents had much value. If we proceeded with the case, our expert might find the file helpful in gaining some background information about the restaurant. Other than that, it contained dull material, regardless of how animated Tony had been during his explanations. Little did I know that almost two years later, this file and Tony's testimony would loom large in the case against Burger King.

13

IT BEGINS

A few weeks after Judge Character found Christopher Martin guilty on all counts, we filed Marie's civil lawsuit in the Cuyahoga County Court of Common Pleas in Cleveland, Ohio, effectively beginning the case against Burger King; Harold Stillwater, the businessman who'd owned the franchise prior to assigning it to his own company; and Quick Eats Enterprises, Inc., the company to which Stillwater had transferred his ownership. Several months earlier, Marie had decided that she did want to pursue a case against the restaurant and had given us permission to proceed. By filing the lawsuit, we were finally in a position to discover all of the facts and try to develop the case.

In the previous few months, we had uncovered what we could. I had talked to Christy Washington and Sheila Williams, the two women who had watched the events unfold from a nearby apartment building. At first both women were reluctant to talk to me, but after I told them how grateful Marie was for their help, they opened up. They estimated that the two men had been loitering in the parking lot for about an hour to an hour and a half, roughly from dusk until the shooting at 6:30. After the shooting, both men had run away, although the tall man had returned to retrieve his car a few minutes later. They had also watched Marie as she staggered out of her car and ran into the restaurant. I thought that when the time came for them to testify at trial, they could be compelling eyewitnesses.

I'd also called Detective Nowak and Brittany Kirkpatrick. Nowak had pledged his cooperation, but at first, my phone messages to Brittany had gone unreturned. Finally, after I sent her a letter, I did hear back from her. After the incident, she had moved back home with her parents in Amherst, Ohio, and my letter had been forwarded to her new address. As it turned out, she now lived within five minutes of my office.

We met there late one afternoon after she had returned home from work. Tall and thin, Brittany was a fair-skinned woman with dark hair who appeared to be in her twenties. As I told her about our firm's involvement in Marie's claim, she asked questions that showed that she was articulate and intelligent.

"I doubt I'd ever file a lawsuit and relive that night over and over again," she said, her body shuddering at the thought. "But I'm curious, do you think they're responsible for what happened to me too?"

"It's possible, but it would depend on how many criminal incidents occurred there before you were abducted. We just don't know that right now, but we'll get that information after we file the lawsuit and get their records," I said.

"You know it's easy to blame yourself for going to that restaurant at night," she said. "But I just thought that a big restaurant chain like that would make their restaurants safe wherever they're located."

Unlike Marie, she'd let the two men into her car after one had pointed a gun at her neck. "Afterwards, I was sure they were going to kill me. They hadn't bothered to wear masks or anything so I'd seen their faces." Her voice began to shake. "I figured that would be reason enough to kill me." She was gripping her hands tightly in her lap and looking down at her feet. For a moment, I thought she was going to cry. "Thank God, one of them took charge and let me go."

"Your testimony is very important to us," I said. "When those same men abducted you at Burger King, it put the restaurant on notice that it had to do something quickly. And we don't think they did anything at all. We really need you to come into the courtroom and tell your story."

"I'll do it," she said without hesitation. "This should be easier than testifying at the criminal trial. Then I was scared that someone connected to the defendant, a family member or friend, would try to harm me before the trial. That won't happen this time."

I thanked her and told her we would be in touch.

We'd also secured crime statistics for the immediate area from the Cleveland Police Department. The census tract records disclosed more than 1,645 criminal incidents within blocks of the restaurant for the year preceding Marie's incident.

With the filing of this lawsuit, the restaurant's internal business records would be discoverable for the first time. We'd also be able to question its employees and other witnesses under oath in a deposition. The defendants would also seek information from us and would take depositions of Marie and our witnesses.

Marie's civil lawsuit would allow her to seek money damages for all that had happened to her—from her medical bills and lost wages to her permanent impairments and pain. To win, we needed to show that the restaurant had been negligent by failing to provide adequate security to its customers. I knew that money was not Marie's motivation for the lawsuit, but it was the engine that would drive the defendants to take responsibility and make changes.

The lawsuit had also included a claim for punitive damages, a type of damage that is designed to punish a defendant for bad conduct. In this case, we believed these damages were warranted if, in fact, the defendants had shut their eyes and failed to make any changes after the earlier incident.

Chuck also had a claim based on his wife's injuries, and we included him in the lawsuit. Although Chuck had initially been cool to the idea of a lawsuit, he'd soon understood that this case was very important to Marie. He'd also witnessed her suffering and struggle after each surgery and had gradually come to realize that she would always carry physical and emotional scars from the shooting. He'd always respected his wife's determination and willingness to fight for things she believed in. After all she'd been through, he would stand with her.

A few weeks after the lawsuit had been filed, I received a phone call from the attorney representing the franchisee, Quick Eats Enterprises, and Harold Stillwater. As was customary, he was seeking permission to extend the time to file his answer, something I routinely granted to other attorneys. These phone calls are a good way for attorneys who have never dealt with one another to introduce themselves. It can also be a time to fish for information, plant a seed about a defense or claim, or simply build a rapport with opposing counsel—something that is useful later when we schedule depositions and request documents. Although opposing attorneys represent different parties, litigation goes much more smoothly when they proceed in a spirit of cooperation.

The attorney's name was John Rasmussen. Although he and the other attorneys in his firm had an office in Lakewood, they were actually employees of Liberty Mutual Insurance Company and defended cases when their insured customers were sued in the Cleveland area. The restaurant in question was insured by Liberty Mutual, thus his involvement.   ·

"We know about the incident, but we don't know much about Mrs. Grossman's injuries," he began.

I provided him with a summary of both her injuries and her limitations and told him that she had not yet completed all of her treatment. "What can you tell me about Harold Stillwater?" I asked.

Rasmussen said, "I just met with him a few days ago. He's rather upset about the lawsuit, as you might guess."

I didn't respond.

"He's a devout Christian. I guess you'd call him a born-again Christian," Rasmussen continued. "He felt called to put a restaurant in this inner-city neighborhood and provide employment for the young people who lived there. From what I gather, he's a very generous man."

Although I was surprised to hear this, I didn't feel any particular sympathy for Mr. Stillwater. Unlike Marie, he hadn't been victimized in a criminal attack. Despite his alleged philanthropic motive for operating the restaurant, I suspected that he turned a profit at this location. Rasmussen's comment did hint at a way he could spin this story to the jury: Stillwater had taken an economic risk to invest in the inner city and provide jobs to its residents. He'd maintain that his unfortunate client had been sued for an incident that neither he nor the police could have prevented.

Not knowing how to respond, I decided to change the subject.

"So how did you end up doing insurance defense work?" I asked. "You know, that's what I did for seven years myself."

I often interjected my insurance background to create a bridge with opposing counsel. I, too, had walked in their shoes and knew the difficulties they faced in convincing their insurance "overlords" to follow their advice. We had represented about eight insurance companies when I'd first started at the firm, but after my father's death in 1985, we'd decided to severe our ties with them, much to their shock. Our natural sympathies were with the injured people, not the insurance companies, whose loyalty was never assured, particularly after an internal reorganization brought in new decision-makers. We also relished the David-and-Goliath struggles that often characterized disputes with them. It was much more fun being the underdog.

Rasmussen chuckled before he answered my question. "I got an interview with Liberty Mutual's office in Florida through my brother-in-law, who was an attorney down there. I came dressed in a navy-blue suit, white shirt, and red tie, and did my best during the interview—I did okay, but I was a little nervous. When my interview was over, the managing attorney, who'd conducted the interview, introduced me to three other attorneys who were in the break room playing cards during their lunch hour. One of them said to me, 'Hey, do you play hearts?' I'd played my fair share during law school and told them so. One of the other guys said, 'You've got to hire this kid because we need a fourth.' I joined them in the card game and a few days later got the job. I moved up to Cleveland a few years later when a position opened up here. You see, my wife was from Northeast Ohio, and she really wanted to come home and be near her family. We had three kids by then."

I laughed. Unlike some defense attorneys, who could be a bit stuffy, this one had a self-deprecating sense of humor. He could also tell a good story and would relate well to jurors. We talked some more about our backgrounds and learned that we were both thirty-five years old and had been practicing for ten years.

I told him that I had paper discovery ready to be sent to him. Before depositions were scheduled, both sides usually sent out requests for documents and written questions that the clients would be required to answer under oath. We kept our requests simple, limiting questions to identifying ownership, the restaurant's hours of operation, the names of employees on duty at the time of Marie's shooting, whether the restaurant routinely employed a security guard at the restaurant, and other similar questions. Theoretically, clients were supposed to answer these questions with help from their attorney, but in reality, the attorney answered the questions and later had the client verify the answers. When we wanted the details, we'd take depositions from their clients, who would be on their own—and more likely to reveal damaging information.

We learned a lot about opposing counsel by the way they responded to the written discovery. Some attorneys stonewalled by objecting to almost all the requests for information. They would stamp a boilerplate objection to each request, claiming that it was either overly broad, irrelevant, or undiscoverable because of a confidentiality exemption. When this happened, we had to seek an order from the court to obtain the information, which was both maddening and time-consuming. On the other hand, others lawyers sent the requested information voluntarily, knowing that the rules required potential evidence to be exchanged freely between all parties, regardless of who possessed it.

A few days later, Ben received a call from another attorney, Frank Soldat, who was representing Burger King. Frank headed the Cleveland law office for Travelers Insurance. Frank and several other attorneys defended all of the local lawsuits brought against individuals and businesses insured by Travelers. Ben knew Frank well; they had worked together at Travelers and been in the same class at Cleveland-Marshall College of Law.

Frank had been a mathematician but had changed professions when he tired of being a professor at Case Western Reserve University. He had a wry sense of humor and was well liked by his attorney colleagues, but he did not always connect with the average juror. As is often the case with the very bright, he could also be somewhat absentminded, particularly with his dress—which did not always involve a matching color scheme. He was, however, a straight shooter.

Ben walked into my office and sat down. "I just got off the phone with Frank Soldat. Travelers insures Burger King, and so he's got their defense. He said to tell you thanks for including him in the lawsuit, but he's not paying anything on the claim—ever."

"Really. That's pretty smug, even before we've done any discovery."

"You know Frank. He's got his marching orders from Travelers and is just communicating the company's position. He says Burger King does not run the restaurant in question. It's all in the hands of the franchisee, Quick Eats Enterprises, and this guy Harold Stillwater. If Burger King doesn't have any say on how to run the restaurant, he claims that they're not liable."

"Well, that's not the test," I answered.

"I know," Ben said. "I told him it's whether they have a right to control. It's not whether they're dictating every move at the restaurant; it's whether they have retained some control and can object or overrule some procedure."

"What did he say to that?"

"He says even if they had some joint control over something, Stillwater signed an agreement that he would indemnify Burger King if they ever were hit with damages in a lawsuit arising out of this restaurant. You can get a judgment against Burger King, but Stillwater's insurance company will have to pay it, not Burger King or Travelers."

"Interesting," I said.

"He also says that he's going to file a motion for summary judgment and get dismissed from the lawsuit for those reasons."

In almost any important case, motions for summary judgment were a common obstacle thrown in our path. The party filing the motion usually alleged that even if the facts were construed in the plaintiff's favor, the law didn't allow a recovery. The defendant's supporting brief always cited cases where courts had denied recovery under similar fact patterns. Our job was to show that the facts weren't as the defendant claimed. We'd also argue that there were other cases that supported our position.

We wanted to keep as many defendants in the lawsuit as possible for a variety of reasons. Sometimes the defendants would start fighting among themselves and point fingers at one another—something we loved to sit back and watch. But in the end, if Marie intended to influence the way Burger King did business, Burger King had to remain in the case. It was that simple.

About a month later, I unexpectedly learned more about Harold Stillwater. While at a party, I met a man who had worked for him for several years before moving on to another job.

"He's a real contradiction. He can be a hard-nosed businessman at times or extremely generous. He might refuse to pay a vendor for some technical reason but go home that evening, clear out the family pantry, and donate it all to a food bank the next day."

I nodded, taking it all in.

"He's a former marine. Although he doesn't go around saying 'Semper Fi' all the time, when he gives an order, he expects it to be obeyed," the man said without laughing. "He likes things done his way. He believes that he knows more than the corporate big shots and was always arguing with Burger King about its marketing campaigns."

"What else can you tell me?" I asked, pressing him.

"Here's vintage Harold. I was in the car with him one day when he picked up a hitchhiker. The man gave us his hard-luck story. When

Harold dropped him off, he reached into his pocket and handed the man a wad of bills, probably several hundred dollars. That's just the way he was—sometimes a hard-as-nails businessman and, at other times, prone to spontaneous acts of charity. He treated me very well, but, of course, I worked my tail off for him."

I didn't know if any of this would ever be useful in our case, but I'd file it away for future reference. The owner had a strong personality with an undeniable charitable streak, perhaps someone that a jury would really like. We'd need to keep this in mind. However, Harold Stillwater would not be calling the shots in our lawsuit. Liberty Mutual, his insurance carrier, had complete control over the defense of the case.

Four months after we'd filed the lawsuit, both defendants provided answers to our written questions and request for documents. Neither defense attorney played hardball, and accordingly, they provided much of the requested information, some of which made our case more difficult.

The owners did hire off-duty policemen to serve as security guards, usually from 7:30 p.m. to 9:30 p.m. most days. We could not argue that this Burger King's management was indifferent to criminal threats and failed to protect its employees and customers. However, the guards' hours seemed very limited for a restaurant whose dining room opened at 6 a.m. every morning and closed at 9 p.m. In addition, its drive-thru stayed open until midnight, during which time, apparently, no one monitored the parking lot to discourage criminal activity. Still, the case would have been much easier if the restaurant had not hired any security guards.

On the other hand, the documents showed that the owner knew that its customers and employees were vulnerable to criminal attacks there. We'd requested incident reports for the past seven years involving Stillwater's Burger King restaurants in the greater Cleveland area, all fifteen of them. We wanted to compare the restaurant in question to all the others. If it stood out as the one most likely to attract criminal activity, then we would be able to argue that extra security measures were required there. Although the Burger King at East Eighty-Fifth and Euclid, known as Restaurant No. 1173, had more criminal activity than any other location, we were surprised that there hadn't been more incidents.

Several weeks later, John Rasmussen called to apologize about their responses. He'd discovered that his client hadn't turned over all of the incident reports to him. When he had sought police reports from the Cleveland Police Department involving the Burger King in question, he'd received records for additional criminal incidents that were not part of his initial disclosure. Rasmussen had immediately contacted Ron Stillwater, Harold's son, who supervised this restaurant and several others on Cleveland's East Side and who had been responsible for locating and sending the documents to him. Even after speaking with Ron Stillwater, Rasmussen still wasn't sure why he hadn't received all of the documents initially. However, once he'd discovered the discrepancy, he'd acted quickly and honorably.

Now that we had a more complete picture of the criminal activity at the restaurant in question, Ben and I spread the incident and police reports on the conference room table. Spanning the seven years before Marie's incident, the reports told of armed robberies of cashiers, fights in the restaurant, and thefts from unoccupied cars in the parking lot. We decided to separate out all of the gun-related crimes on the premises, either inside or out, committed against both employees and customers. When the dust had settled, we'd identified twelve incidents over the past seven years in which employees or customers had been robbed at gunpoint there.

"Let's get some depositions scheduled, particularly management. We'll see if they took any action over the years to increase safety at this Burger King," Ben said.

"It looks like Harold Stillwater's son Ron oversaw operations here. He'd be a place to start."

We also decided to depose all of the employees who were working at the restaurant the night Marie was shot. We hoped that one of these rank-and-file employees might be candid about security at the restaurant, particularly if he or she were no longer employed there.

After receiving this initial information, we now had some basic building blocks, but the next phase, the depositions, would be crucial. What steps had the restaurant taken to increase security? How did they determine when to post security guards on the property? Did the guards stay exclusively inside or did they also patrol the grounds? Did the restaurant have video monitoring of the premises? Were employees trained to detect and deal with loiterers? We'd soon get those answers.

We had to demonstrate not only that the restaurant could have done more to provide a safer environment, but that those changes would have been practical and economical. We would soon see.

14

MAKING A STATEMENT

As we began the new year of 1989, the defendants requested Marie's deposition. On a blustery January day, she sat in our conference room to preview the questions that opposing counsel were likely to ask her.

"I doubt that we'll need to spend much time with you today," Ben began. "You know exactly what a deposition is, so no need to explain that. Normally, we tell clients to keep their answers short and not to volunteer information that hasn't been asked, but we think you may be more effective if you give detailed responses. We'll leave that up to you. If you want to be expansive on an answer, go ahead."

Marie nodded her understanding. "I've actually been looking forward to this," she said. Her appearance seemed to mirror that statement. She was wearing a dark-green business suit with a high-collared beige blouse, formal clothes that bespoke confidence.

"That's good," Ben said. "We want them to hear your story directly from you."

"Marie, there are no wrong answers here," I said. "You know what happened to you that evening and all of the treatment and complications that followed. Just tell your story. More than anything, the other attorneys will be trying to determine if you'll be an effective witness—whether you can connect with jurors. They'll gauge this by your answers and demeanor."

"Oh boy, you're putting all the pressure on me," Marie said with a laugh.

"No, just be yourself. That's all," I told her.

"I've tried to think about the types of questions I'll be asked and how I'd respond," she said. From a folder, she pulled out several pages where she'd handwritten a timeline of her medical care and summarized her limitations.

"Normally, we are the ones who prepare this kind of summary," Ben said. "No need to review any of this with you. You've already done it."

"I agree," I said. "But there is one thing that you should be aware of. The defendants have alleged that you were comparatively negligent."

Mare looked shocked. "What? They're claiming that I was negligent and am partially responsible for my own injuries?"

"Yes, that's what they alleged in their answer, but who knows if they're really going to argue that at trial. I can't see a jury buying that at all," I said.

"Have they told you what I supposedly did that was negligent?" Marie asked. I could hear some indignation in her voice.

"No. I've never brought it up and neither has Rasmussen, but he's likely to ask some questions to develop the defense. Insurance companies raise every possible defense, even long shots like this one. They probably don't believe in it themselves, but they want to give us something to worry about," I said.

"I had no choice. He didn't take my purse. I offered him the keys to the car. What was I supposed to do? Let him in?" Marie protested.

"Just explain why you did what you did. That should be sufficient," Ben said. "It's a defense that will go nowhere."

"Okay," Marie said. She turned to me as she changed the subject. "You know, I'm not one to back down when I think I'm right, but I'm not out to bankrupt anybody either. That's not why I filed this lawsuit. I'm just trying to make a point. I want them to make their restaurants safer, and I'd like them to acknowledge that they made a mistake in my situation. If they'd taken just a few simple precautions, all this could have been avoided."

"That's what our security expert is saying too," Ben said. "He's seen what we've gathered so far and believes they did a really poor job with security. He's identified four or five areas where their security measures were inadequate, and he'll testify to that at trial."

"Do you think this case will actually proceed to trial?" Marie asked. This was a question that all clients asked, some repeatedly. The problem was that we never knew which cases would settle and which ones wouldn't. Ninety-five percent settled, but when the case was unusual, insurance companies often didn't adequately evaluate their exposure. And Marie's case was novel. In all likelihood, Liberty Mutual had never defended a claim of negligent security nor evaluated an injury involving a gunshot wound through the jaw.

"It's too early to tell at this point," Ben said. "We'll have a better idea after all of the depositions have been taken and we get a report from your surgeon, Dr. Zins, about your permanent limitations."

* * *

The mood was somber the next morning as Marie sat directly across from John Rasmussen, who was absorbed in reviewing the questions he'd outlined on a yellow pad. He would begin asking them in a few minutes. With her fingers interlaced and her hands resting on the table, Marie looked confident. Ben sat next to her and I next to him. Across from us, Frank Soldat, Burger King's lawyer, and a Liberty Mutual adjuster named Andy Wargo whispered to one another.

Explaining that his goal was to learn more about her claim, Rasmussen told her that if his questions were not clear and straightforward, then she should let him know. Before inquiring about the incident at Burger King, Rasmussen delved into her background, focusing on her education and prior work experience as an attorney. He also wanted to know about her husband's company, what products it manufactured, and how large it was. This was more than just idle curiosity. If he wanted to build a barrier between Marie and the working-class jurors who would hear her case, these facts could be the foundation.

Although I'd heard Marie recount the events at Burger King several times, it was always a powerful narrative. As she told her story that morning, the defense attorneys stopped writing notes, set down their pens, and simply listened. Marie had the ability to break down the events into the minutest detail and to allow the listener to enter her mind as she recalled her thoughts. Her story drew them in just as I'd known it would.

She paused after she told them about the gun firing and knowing that she had been shot in the head. Rasmussen asked, "Was the gun in his right hand?"

"Yes."

"Was his right hand and arm inside the window when you hit the accelerator?"

"Yes, it was, but I didn't 'hit' the accelerator; I pressed on it."

"Did you consider that his right hand—let's call it his gun hand—would suddenly strike the door pillar when the car moved forward?"

For the first time, Marie hesitated before answering. She took a deep breath and slowly said, "No."

Rasmussen looked down at his yellow pad and flipped through several pages. Before he could ask another question, Marie continued. "I had just a few seconds to decide what to do. He didn't want my purse or the keys to my car. When he tried to push his way into the backseat, I concluded that he wanted me. And here's the picture that flashed in my mind—my dead body being dumped into a vacant lot."

The court reporter, a woman about my age, looked up from her stenographic machine and raised her eyebrows. *So much for the defense of comparative negligence*, I thought.

For the next forty-five minutes, Rasmussen inquired about Marie's hospitalizations and surgeries. As a former insurance defense attorney, I knew that the goal here was to search for some admissions that he could use later to minimize her injuries at trial. I had deposed plaintiffs who had forgotten parts of their treatment or failed to detail all of their injuries—not so with Marie. She led him from the first night in the hospital to her fourth and final surgery just two months ago. Her tone was not melodramatic, angry, or tearful but analytical and informative.

"Let's move to your lost-wage claim," Rasmussen said. "Are you employed now?"

"No, I'm still looking," Marie said.

"Are you claiming that you have been unable to work since the incident?"

"Let me try to explain why I haven't worked. That might be easier. Is that okay?" Marie asked.

"Yes, that would be fine."

"First of all, I have either worked full-time or been a full-time student my entire adult life except for 1971 and 1972, when my second son was born. Throughout 1988, I had multiple surgeries, each of which required a recovery period. My face was often swollen and bruised, and until I had speech therapy, I did not feel confident with my speaking abilities. I had many doctor and physical therapy appointments and daily jaw and facial exercises. Through June of 1988, I was involved in the criminal justice system, testifying at the trial of one of the perpetrators. As you know, my last surgery was in November of 1988."

"Did you lose your job at Preferred Health?"

"I couldn't ask them to hold it open for me indefinitely. They needed someone who could work every day—I just couldn't do that. We agreed that they needed to replace me. So yes, I lost that job."

"Have you applied for any jobs?"

"I've updated my résumé and hope to send it out in the next few weeks. You have to remember that the swelling from my last surgery just receded a few weeks ago. According to a recent article in the *Wall Street Journal*, it usually takes about five to six months to find a new job for someone like me. I hope to be employed again soon, and I'm optimistic that it won't take five months. But to answer your question, no, I haven't applied for a new job yet."

"Let's switch gears a bit. You've made significant strides in your recovery; would you agree with that?"

"Yes," Marie answered.

"There are things you couldn't do after the first surgery that you can do now. Correct?"

"Yes," Marie said, but this time there was a wariness in her voice.

"You've just been answering my questions for the last hour and a half. Would you say that your ability to speak has returned to normal?"

"I can be understood, if that's what you mean," she answered. "But it's not the way I used to talk. I can't enunciate all sounds, and I have to speak more slowly. For example, I have trouble saying my own name, especially over the phone. If I don't concentrate, my throat muscles tense and I speak in a higher pitch."

"Has your speech improved over time?"

"Yes. Last year I had speech therapy at Mount Sinai hospital that really helped."

"You've returned to eating solid foods, correct?" he asked.

"Some," Marie answered.

"Tell me what you can't eat."

"Well, I'm afraid that I'm sounding like a complainer. One thing I tell everyone is that I feel very lucky to be alive. I hope you understand that."

Rasmussen smiled. "No one considers you a complainer," he said. "I'm asking you these questions so that my client has a full understanding of your injuries and limitations." He looked over at Andy Wargo, the Liberty Mutual adjuster, who nodded in agreement.

"Let me try to explain. Some foods I can't eat because I can't open my jaw enough. That would be something like a whole banana or a Big Mac hamburger. Other foods I can't extend my lower jaw enough to bite into it. I can't eat a whole apple, for instance. My jaw doesn't move laterally, and I can't chew food like lettuce, raw vegetables, rice, and other foods that require more chewing. Do you want me to go into the problems I have with eating too?"

"Yes, please do that."

"I have lost the sense of taste except in the back of my tongue. Crackers taste like gravel. The most embarrassing part is that I can't chew with my mouth closed. As a result, liquid slips out when I chew cantaloupe or pineapple. I can't drink without drooling. To compensate, I put my finger under my lip. I'm now extra sensitive to icy things. I can't feel food on my chin because of nerve damage. Because I can't chew as well, I choke more often and I have to be really careful."

Ben slid his yellow pad across the table so that I could see it. He had drawn a large arrow pointing upward. It was his way of telling me that Marie was doing extremely well.

"Are there foods that you don't eat because of this?"

"Here are the ones that come to mind: ice-cream cones, tossed salads, raw vegetables, corn on the cob, pizza, fried chicken, most meats, crackers, peanuts, popcorn, most cookies, and almost all sandwiches. I used to love to eat, so this has been a big adjustment for me."

None of the defense attorneys or the adjuster showed any emotion, but they had to be concerned. Marie was unusually adept at explaining how her injuries impacted her daily life in a way that jurors could understand. Yet, she was not portraying herself as a victim, but as someone who had made significant adjustments to do ordinary things that the rest of us took for granted.

"Do you claim to have sustained any emotional damage?" Rasmussen asked.

"I relive that night every day. It was a moment of sheer terror."

"Does it affect how you live your life?"

"Of course. I live with these feelings of vulnerability and insecurity. I panic whenever a stranger approaches my car. My husband will tell you that I'm obsessive about locking doors, particularly car doors. I've wanted to buy a gun to protect myself, but I haven't bought one yet because my husband is absolutely against it."

"Anything else?"

"I've experienced a loss of confidence. I don't know how best to explain it. I'm a different person now. I used to be healthy, employed, and always in control of my life. I'm not any of those things anymore. Right now, I feel as if I'm living with a disability. Would I like to be the person I was before the shooting? Absolutely. I'm just not there yet."

"Thank you, Mrs. Grossman. I don't have any more questions for you."

15

BUILDING THE CASE

I could tell that Mylayna Albright was nervous as her deposition began. Almost one year before, the eighteen-year-old had listened as Marie Grossman had placed her food order at the Burger King drive-thru. Well-groomed, Mylayna sat with her hands folded beneath the table's surface. She surveyed our conference table, where two other attorneys and a court reporter stared back at her. I tried to put her at ease by explaining the ground rules for her deposition and asked her to stop me if at any time she did not understand the question. She said that she would.

After questioning her about her background, I asked her what she remembered about the evening of December 11, 1987.

"I want you to know that I will never forget that evening. It bothers me very much."

"In what ways?" I asked.

"It haunts me, and sometimes I have nightmares. I hear the gunshot in the parking lot, and then I see the woman running into the restaurant. She's holding her face together and bleeding where she was shot. She's dripping blood onto the floor as she gets to the counter and grabs the order pad. I can't get that out of my head," she said, her voice trembling for the first time.

"Do you want to take a break?" I asked.

"No, I just want to get this over with," she replied.

For the next few minutes, we discussed the events leading up to the shooting. She recalled that it was a quiet evening with few customers—

unusual for a Friday night. The dining room was almost empty when Mrs. Grossman pulled up to the menu board. After Mrs. Grossman placed an order for chicken tenders, there was a pause. Mylayna was about to ask her if she had completed her order when a loud pop came through the speaker.

"Did you have video cameras pointed toward the menu board?"

"No."

"Were there any video cameras on the premises?"

"We had one in the restaurant, and it was directed toward the front counter and the cash register."

"Do you know why it was pointed to that area of the restaurant?"

"I'm not sure, but Mr. Wagner—he used to be the manager—he said the camera would catch anyone if they tried to steal from the register or give away free hamburgers to their friends."

"Were there any cameras that were directed toward either the front or back parking lot?"

"Not that I know."

"Do they have any now?" I asked.

"Objection," Rasmussen said. I could ask this question in deposition, where most anything is fair game as long as it might lead to relevant and admissible evidence down the road. However, this same question would not be allowed during the trial. Evidence of a defendant's "subsequent remedial repair," as it was known in legalese, could not be used to prove the defendant's negligence. Although relevant, this information was kept from the jury because it theoretically discouraged a potential defendant from immediately making a repair after a loss if that action could be used against it later. The law encouraged repairs and changes that made things safer. However, the question was proper during a deposition.

"You can answer," I said to the witness. "Mr. Rasmussen was just protecting the record."

Mylayna looked confused and glanced at Rasmussen. He nodded to her that she could proceed. "It's just a technical thing that I had to do," he explained to her.

"I don't know if they made any changes," Mylayna replied.

"Why is that?" I asked.

"Because I quit this job two weeks after this incident, and I've never been back." She looked down at the table and repositioned herself on her chair.

"Why did you quit?" I asked.

"Well, you see, the restaurant opens at 6 a.m. for breakfast, and sometimes I had to work right when it opened," Mylayna said, suddenly turning herself toward the court reporter as if she felt compelled to explain things specifically to her. "It was dark when I arrived that early, and without a security guard present, I just didn't feel safe."

Mylayna had just presented our case with an unexpected gift. Unknown to her, she had summarized one of our security expert's conclusions—at a minimum, a security guard needed to be actively working on the premises whenever it was dark. I could have asked her to explain her answer further, but I resisted the urge. I'd received a good answer and decided to stop. If I pushed her further, she could retreat and claim that her fear was based on the absence of people in the early morning. I'd learned the hard way (and more than once) that an extra question could erase a witness's damaging admission. I moved on.

"Let's talk a bit about the security guards," I said. "When were they present?"

"Usually around closing. Maybe an hour or so before we shut down the dining room at nine o'clock."

"What did you see them do?"

"They'd stay near the door of the dining room or walk around inside. They talked to some of the customers from time to time. Sometimes they'd sit down and drink a cup of coffee. That kind of stuff."

"Did they go outside and patrol the parking lot on a regular basis?"

"I don't know. I really didn't pay that much attention to them," she said. Again, she looked uncomfortable, not wanting to say more.

"When you saw them inside the restaurant, did they take off their outdoor coats?"

"Yes."

"Did you ever see a security guard put on his jacket and go outside to see what was happening?"

"I suppose they did."

"But did you ever see it happen?"

"I just don't remember. I was busy taking orders."

"You certainly did not see them go out regularly, like every ten minutes or so?" I prodded.

"No, they were mainly inside." She paused, and then she seemed to have a new thought. "There was a time when they went outside every night."

"When was that?"

"After we closed the dining room, the guard would go outside with the manager or assistant manager with the night deposit. He definitely went outside then," she said.

"Was this after nine o'clock?" I asked.

"Yes."

"Would you see them again while the drive-thru was open—up until midnight?"

"I'm not sure. I think they were gone. I usually went home right after we closed the dining room. I never worked the drive-thru after 9 p.m., so I don't know for sure."

This witness was giving us a candid glimpse of the restaurant's operation. Was it a coincidence that the video surveillance camera was directed at employees and that the security guard protected the night deposit? We could argue that the security arrangements were geared to protect the restaurant's property and, in particular, its cash—not to safeguard its customers.

As part of our earlier document discovery, Burger King had produced a small book called the Loss Control Manual that included guidelines for security that it sold to franchisees like Stillwater and Quick Eats Enterprises. The book recommended that employees receive training in identifying six types of suspicious activity that ranged from a customer's boisterous behavior to the passing of counterfeit bills. Mylayna did not remember receiving any such training.

I had no further questions for her, and Frank Soldat, Burger King's attorney, opted not to ask her any questions. I could understand his reluctance. We had a full slate of depositions scheduled for the remainder of the day and tomorrow.

Although I had wanted to schedule the employees of Quick Eats Enterprises one after the other, we were forced to depose the two police officers next because of their schedules. Frank Soldat had requested their depositions and questioned both Detective Nowak and Sergeant Philip Meli. I had spoken with Nowak previously and knew how the police had apprehended Marie's assailants. During their depositions, the defense attorneys listened with interest to their intriguing account. I declined to ask them any additional questions.

After lunch, I took the deposition of Ronald Stillwater, the son of Harold Stillwater. Although I had initially wanted to take the elder Stillwater's deposition, Rasmussen explained that Harold Stillwater had virtually nothing to do with the operation of this Burger King restaurant. Instead, his son was identified as the most knowledgeable corporate employee because he supervised this restaurant and the company's other East Side restaurants.

Ron Stillwater was in his late twenties and was neatly dressed in a blue blazer and gray slacks. He looked like a football linebacker, around six feet five inches tall with a muscular, chiseled build. Upon being introduced, we shook hands, although he did not smile.

The younger Stillwater had graduated from a small liberal arts college a few years before. He'd always worked in his father's Burger King restaurants. In high school, he'd started at an entry-level position, and after his graduation from college, he had quickly become a supervisor of four restaurants. I thought I would begin my questioning where I had left off with Mylayna Albright.

"Mr. Stillwater, I'm handing to you what was previously marked as Plaintiff's Exhibit Five, the Loss Control Manual that Burger King sold to franchisees such as Quick Eats Enterprises. Have you ever seen this before?"

Stillwater glanced through the manual and then flipped it back onto the table. "Yeah, I've seen it before."

"Does it have a training section for crew members that involves identifying suspicious behavior in and about the restaurant?"

Stillwater scooped the book off the table and began thumbing through it. "It might," he said.

"Let's turn to page twenty-five and the section that spells out what the franchisee should do to train its employees to identify suspicious behavior. Do you see it?"

"Yes."

"Did you provide this training to your employees?"

"We certainly made our managers and assistant managers aware of these situations."

"Do you see where it recommends that you train your *crew members* about security issues?"

Stillwater shut the book and stared at me for a few seconds before answering. "Mr. Miraldi, when you are running a Burger King in the inner city, your biggest concern is getting the crew members to show up for work. We're trying to develop good work habits with them. You can't throw too much at them."

"So is that a no? You did not provide any security training to crew members at this restaurant."

"That is correct. Not at this restaurant."

"Well, how about at other restaurants?"

"What you have to understand, sir, is that our employees are very young people. Most of them are teenagers. Some are high school drop-outs. It's enough to get them to fill orders quickly and make the correct change. We don't train them to be little detectives at work."

"Is that a no? You don't follow the guidelines in this manual for any of your restaurants?"

"That's a no."

I could see where jurors might sympathize with his plight. The security training sounded important and necessary in the abstract, but in the real world, it could be both impractical and ineffective. I moved to another subject.

"Did you at some point learn that a customer, Brittany Kirkpatrick, had been abducted by two men while ordering at this restaurant's menu board on the evening of October 24, 1987?"

"We found out about it the next day when the police came and investigated. We were very upset that this had happened at our restaurant, and we cooperated with them fully."

"Was there a security guard present when this happened?"

"No."

"Why not?"

"We'd never had anyone accosted at the drive-thru like this before. This happened close to midnight from what I understand. We release the security guard after we take the night deposit out."

"I'm not sure I understand your reason."

"It's unnecessary and expensive. We can't have a security guard present for the eighteen hours the restaurant is open each day when we rarely have a problem there. We have security at the restaurant in the last hour and a half that the restaurant is open. You've got to remember that most of our prior criminal acts were situations where a criminal robbed one of our cashiers. We didn't think that customers had any greater risk in our parking lot than they did on the streets outside the restaurant."

"Did you have any video cameras that monitored activities outside of the restaurant at the time of the Brittany Kirkpatrick incident?"

"No."

"Why not?"

"We didn't believe that they would do much good. If we saw a crime in progress, all we could do was to call the police. By the time the police arrived, the criminal would be gone."

"That's all you would do?"

"In today's world, it's always a pretty good bet that the criminal is carrying a weapon. We would not be sending out any of our employees to stop him and put their lives at risk. We wouldn't direct our security guard to confront them either. We don't want a shoot-out at the restaurant. That would be a real disaster."

"Wouldn't cameras have a deterrent effect? Criminals would go elsewhere to do their crime?"

"That assumes that they were that careful. I don't know that cameras discourage criminal behavior."

"Did you do anything differently after Brittany Kirkpatrick's abduction to increase security for restaurant customers in any way?"

"We were kicking around some ideas, yes."

"Such as?"

"We were pricing out video cameras. We were thinking about increasing the hours for our security guards."

"But none of those changes had been accomplished?"

"Right."

"Did you hire anyone to conduct a study and make recommendations about reducing risks to customers and employees?"

"No." He paused for a moment as if finished, then continued. "You know, the two guys that committed these crimes also did the same thing at Popeyes and McDonald's and other fast-food restaurants in the area. Nobody else was able to stop them either. We weren't the only place where they struck."

"So there was no use in trying to improve security?"

"I'm not saying that. You had two guys who did this for about three months. Since they've been caught, this hasn't happened again at any of the restaurants. It's not that all the restaurants have increased their security; it's that the bad guys are behind bars now. That's what I'm saying. If somebody came onto our property with a gun tomorrow, who knows what crimes he might commit? We can't prevent everything."

Because jurors are not present during depositions, lawyers often let witnesses go off on a rant—hoping that they may hang themselves. Stillwater hadn't done that. On the contrary, he'd made arguments that could resonate with jurors. At trial, we would not give him this opportunity. If any of his answers became unresponsive, we'd stop him and have the judge admonish him to simply answer the question posed.

Today was a different matter. Lawyers primarily use depositions to tie down a witness's story. If their account at trial differs in any significant way, the attorney will confront them with their earlier inconsistent statement. When this happens, witnesses usually lose their credibility with the jury. The witness's personality is also revealed during deposition. Do they exaggerate? Do they have a temper? Do they talk too much? Do they guess? I'd learned a few things about Ron Stillwater's personality and would now be able to gauge his effectiveness as a witness. However, before I concluded my questioning, I wanted him to answer my original question.

"Just so I have this correctly: the restaurant took no additional steps to increase safety or security at the restaurant after the Brittany Kirkpatrick incident and before the incident with Marie Grossman?"

"No, we hadn't," Stillwater said, his voice edgy and slightly indignant.

The afternoon was getting late when Jack Artman was called as the day's last witness. Artman was a trim man in his fifties who appeared upset that he had waited in our lobby most of the afternoon prior to his testimony. He was Burger King's regional representative for Northeast Ohio and had no affiliation with Harold Stillwater or Quick Eats Enterprises.

He had one objective today: to demonstrate that Burger King had relinquished complete control over this restaurant to its franchisee. If he could maintain that position, Burger King would seek to be dismissed through a motion for summary judgment.

I started by asking about the Loss Control Manual that Burger King had sold to Quick Eats Enterprises. We wanted him to confirm that the manual did not address customer safety and security. Our expert had already told us that it should have.

Handing the manual to Artman, I asked him to review the section that dealt with training employees to prevent losses.

"Mr. Artman, the manual discusses several areas in which employees can be trained to reduce losses at the restaurant, is that right?"

"Yes."

"It discusses ways to provide security for employees and to safeguard restaurant property, does it not?"

"Yes, it does."

"I don't see where your manual makes any recommendations to make the premises safer for customers."

Artman picked up the manual and seemed to be skimming through some pages. "Not directly, no."

"Does it make some recommendations in an indirect way? For example, the manual recommends that the dumpster be locked. Does this improve safety for customers?"

"No."

"What about identifying counterfeit bills? Does this improve customer safety?"

"No."

"Rather than have me read through the list, please tell me how any of these guidelines enhances security for customers."

He was silent for a few moments. "Each restaurant is in a unique location. We, meaning Burger King, can't provide any general guidelines on how a restaurant operator can make its restaurant safer for customers. They have to do that on their own."

"Okay, so none of these recommendations increase security for customers, even indirectly?"

"Well, like I said, that's up to the franchisee, not us."

"Despite Burger King's wide experience, it is unwilling to provide any guidance in security—is that what you're telling me?"

"We can't generalize about security."

"And it's not in your manual."

"No, it's not."

Was Burger King negligent by failing to address security and customer safety in its manual? I wasn't sure, but it might be enough to
keep Burger King in the lawsuit and defeat its motion for summary
judgment. I turned next to the issue of control between Burger King
and its franchisees. We had to show that Burger King retained some
control over its franchised restaurants to hold them responsible for the
franchisee's actions.

"Let's talk about Burger King restaurants. Some are owned by Burger King and some are owned by franchisees like Harold Stillwater,
correct?"

"Yes, we do have company-owned restaurants, but this one was not."

"Well then, how does a customer know which restaurant is owned
and run by Burger King and which is owned by a franchisee?"

"I'm not sure I understand the question."

"Is there some difference in the restaurants? Do they sell different
products? Do they have different building designs? Is there some dis-
claimer that Burger King does not operate a particular restaurant?"

"No, there's no difference. They look the same. They sell the same
meals."

"A customer would expect the same quality in both types of restaurants, correct?"

"I suppose so, yes. We try to make sure that the franchisees stick to
our formula."

"There is a formula that franchisees have to follow, isn't there?"

"Yes."

"There's a franchise agreement and manual that dictates that the
franchisee follows Burger King's standards?"

"Of course."

I then listed some of the standards. They included things like the
temperature of the hamburgers, the cleaning and maintenance of the
parking lot, the training of employees, and the placement of the menu
board.

"Doesn't Burger King have the right to terminate a franchise if the
franchise owner doesn't follow these standards?" I asked.

"I've never seen it done, ever," he replied.

"But if the violations were serious enough and lasted long enough,
Burger King could pull the franchise, right? Under the franchise agreement, they have the right to do this."

"I don't know," he said. "If we did, that could be a long, drawn-out court battle."

If we were in front of a jury, I would have shown him the franchise agreement and turned to the provisions that dealt with franchise revocation, but this was a deposition. There was no jury present. We'd connect the dots later when it really mattered.

16

THE TRIAL APPROACHES

In May of 1989, we received the report from our security expert, Rick Newman. By then we'd deposed the franchisee's comptroller as well as the restaurant's manager and two assistant managers. Based in Houston, Texas, Rick Newman was forty-five years old and had spent his entire work life in the security field. Early in his career, he'd supervised security services and personnel for his employers. Over the past ten years, he'd focused primarily on consulting work, providing security analyses for retail stores, hotels, and restaurants. During that time, he'd also evaluated security issues for attorneys in cases like ours.

Before writing the report, he'd flown to Cleveland, met with us, and visited the Burger King in question. He was a trim, athletic-appearing man with short-cropped brown hair who looked like a law enforcement officer or a career military man. Because so much of our case was riding on his opinions, Ben and I wanted to talk with him in person to evaluate his effectiveness as an expert witness. He'd seemed knowledgeable and answered our questions with authority, but we had no idea how well he'd hold up to a full-scale cross-examination at trial.

Even when an expert remained calm during cross-examination and skillfully parried the questions, the defense could still discredit him later during its closing argument, labeling him a Monday-morning quarterback. Throughout a trial, the defense routinely reminded the jury that almost anything was preventable in hindsight, but things were not so easily avoided as they happened. They'd also emphasize that the plaintiff had paid the expert a fee for his report, calling into question the objectivity and ultimate value of his opinions.

Newman's consulting company was called Security Associates International. We did not question whether his firm actually had worldwide business as its name suggested. To us, the name sounded impressive, and we hoped (perhaps unrealistically) it would to a jury as well.

Newman concluded that both the franchisee and Burger King had failed to exercise ordinary care in providing a secure environment for their customers—in other words, they were negligent. As we'd hoped, he said that the owner should have employed a security guard whenever it was dark—two hours a day was not sufficient. The restaurant should also have installed closed-circuit television cameras to monitor activities on the premises for all hours of operation. Fencing and other barriers should have been erected around the perimeter to limit access to the property. He also took issue with the defendants' failure to provide employee training sessions that would have taught them to identify loiterers and other suspicious behavior. In an opinion directed only against Burger King, he criticized its failure to provide any guidance or regulation regarding security measures in its operation manuals.

When all of the attorneys met with the judge's staff attorney a few months later at a pretrial settlement conference, neither defendant offered any money to settle the case, notwithstanding Newman's report. Speaking first, Rasmussen told us that Liberty Mutual was still evaluating the case and that it might make an offer before trial. But for now, he defended the case as we had predicted: the act was unforeseeable, business owners weren't required to protect customers from every possible contingency, and Richard Thompson's criminal act was the sole cause of Marie's injuries. He dressed up his argument in legalese—concepts like superseding, intervening cause, and lack of foreseeability—but it was the same refrain that had been used for decades to defend these cases.

After Rasmussen explained his clients' position, the staff attorney turned to Frank Soldat. Soldat told the group that Travelers had not changed its position. Burger King did not operate this restaurant, and even if it had exercised some control, it was entitled to be indemnified by the franchisee. I could sense that Ben was disappointed, but instead of arguing with Soldat, he smiled and needled his former law school classmate.

"Come on, Frank, after all we've been through together and you can't get your client to contribute?" Ben said. "What kind of friend are you, anyway?"

The staff attorney looked puzzled by the comments, but Frank was ready with an explanation. Turning to me, Frank said, "David, what you don't know is that when Ben and I were in night law school together at Cleveland-Marshall, we would occasionally—and I stress 'occasionally'—skip out of our classes and go to Northfield Park and bet on the horses. Your partner is indebted to me, not the other way around. As a mathematician, I had this system worked out so we always went home with more money than what we came with."

"Until we lost it all," Ben said.

"Details," Frank replied. "By the way, here's our motion for summary judgment. If the judge follows the law, we should be dismissed from the case." He smiled as he handed the brief to Ben.

I'd known that Ben and Frank had worked together at Travelers in the early 1960s, but I hadn't realized that they had been such good friends during law school. It obviously didn't make any difference now. Each had a client to represent and that was that.

Returning us to the matter at hand, the staff attorney cleared his throat. "Okay, there's not much more for me to do but give you a trial date." He looked at the judge's trial schedule and asked us if our calendars were free beginning on October 2, 1989. He explained that Judge James Kilcoyne, the judge assigned to our case, would probably not try the case because of his backlog of criminal trials. If Judge Kilcoyne was not available, the case would be transferred to a visiting judge who would preside at the trial.

"Make sure that this date is open on your calendars, gentlemen, because there will be no continuances. This case will be tried on that date, if not by Judge Kilcoyne, then by one of our retired visiting judges."

Ben and I left the courthouse convinced that the insurance companies were not reasonably evaluating their exposure. Although we could never predict what any particular jury would do with this case, we thought it more likely that most would rule in our favor. If they did, it was an open question whether they would award a large verdict. A jury might hesitate to give full damages when the defendants were not the actual people who'd directly caused the injuries. In three months, we'd find out.

17

THE DAY BEFORE

All attorneys sat in the chambers of Judge Robert Lawther, the visiting judge who had been assigned the case after Judge Kilcoyne transferred the case out of his busy docket. Before the transfer, Judge Kilcoyne had denied Burger King's motion to be dismissed and Quick Eats Enterprises' motion to strike our claim for punitive damages. All claims would now be decided by a jury. Although the trial would begin the next day, the new judge reserved the morning to acquaint himself with the case, the attorneys, and the status of negotiations.

When a trial was imminent, most Cuyahoga County civil cases in the 1980s were transferred out of the docket of the elected judge and assigned to one of eight visiting judges, former elected judges who had either retired or not sought reelection. As a result of this status, these judges could be appointed to preside over individual trials. As attorneys, we never knew which of the eight would handle our case. Although judges are supposed to show no partiality, some visiting judges seemed to favor the plaintiff, while others were more partial to the defense. Our draw had been a lucky one. Judge Lawther, well liked by both sides, was prone to agree with the plaintiff on close questions of law and admissibility of evidence.

Judge Lawther, the sixty-two-year-old former mayor of Lakewood, had been serving as a visiting judge for about a year after serving two six-year terms as a common pleas judge. Understanding people and motivating them to work toward common goals, he'd accomplished much in both his civic and his public life. He was an outgoing, friendly jurist but could be demanding in the courtroom. He wanted attorneys to be punctual, and if an attorney was not ready to start at exactly the time set for the morning or afternoon session, his irritation was palpable.

Like most judges, he pushed the parties to reach settlements—a result that allowed both sides to claim some semblance of victory. As a general rule, plaintiffs suffered the most when a jury ruled against them: they would get nothing and no second chance. On the other hand, when an insured defendant lost, the insurance company had endless other cases on the horizon where it could even the score. After setting forth some ground rules for his courtroom, Judge Lawther asked us where we were in settlement discussions.

"Not very far," Ben answered.

"Liberty Mutual does have some money to offer the plaintiff," Rasmussen interjected.

"How about you, Frank?" the judge asked Burger King's attorney.

"No. It's not our restaurant. Sole responsibility lies with the franchisee," Soldat replied.

"Gee, I thought the restaurant had your name on it," the judge said, needling him. "Anyway, let me talk to each side individually and see if this case can be resolved. Do we have the parties present and the insurance representatives as I requested?"

We all indicated that this was the case. Judge Lawther spoke with both defense attorneys and their insurance representatives separately and then called us in.

"I doubt you'll be interested in the offer. Liberty Mutual is offering $150,000 to resolve the case, and Travelers is not making any offer."

"That's barely our client's medical bills and lost wages," Ben replied. "We'll take our chances with the jury."

"I figured as much," the judge replied. "The insurance companies are calling the shots here, and they just don't think that a jury will award damages against a restaurant for a criminal act that occurred on its property. The defense attorneys will be telling the jury that the bad guys who did this are in prison and they're the only ones responsible."

"We think we have pretty compelling facts. These same two guys abducted another customer just six weeks before our incident, and the restaurant owners did nothing to try and make the place safer," Ben said. "I'd be concerned if I were the claims people looking at this case."

"Are you looking for a million dollars?" the judge asked.

"We'd take less than that," Ben said. "We're aware that there's a chance that a jury could find no negligence and our client would get nothing—so we have to calculate that into our evaluation. We're confident that the jurors would agree with us, but there's an outside chance that they wouldn't."

After the judge dismissed the attorneys, we brought Marie into the empty courtroom to brief her on the morning's events.

"This is where your trial will be," Ben began. When the case was assigned to a visiting judge, it automatically switched its venue from the Justice Center to the former Cuyahoga County Courthouse across the street. The old courthouse was a beautiful Beaux Arts building constructed at the turn of the twentieth century. Unlike the impersonal Justice Center, the former courthouse's interior dazzled with its marble floors, high ceilings, and dark ornate wainscoting.

Marie glanced around the courtroom before returning her gaze to Ben. "I gather that we're going forward tomorrow," she said with no trace of disappointment in her voice.

"Yes. It's like we expected. They're not willing to accept responsibility for what happened," Ben replied. "The franchisee, through its insurance company, offered $150,000. We recommend that you reject the offer."

"I agree," Marie said. "I'd rather have a jury rule against me and get nothing than to take that. As I've said all along, they need to accept responsibility for what happened to me and what will happen to others if they don't make things safer. As far as I'm concerned, that offer tells me that they don't think they did anything wrong. If that's all they'll pay, then they won't make any security changes either."

"Good. We're all in agreement. We'll see you and Chuck tomorrow at 8:30, right here," Ben said. "We'll start at 9 a.m. and begin picking a jury immediately."

"Yes, we'll be here," Marie said as we parted.

18

DAY ONE

As attorneys wait for a trial to actually begin, they are like Thoroughbred horses bumping around in their starting gates. They worry about the trial preparations that they failed to finish or the witness who is likely to veer off course. They scrutinize the prospective-juror questionnaires and hope that they'll pick the ones who will be receptive to their case. They fret about the evidence that the other side will try to exclude. While all of this is churning away in their heads, they try to appear calm and confident to opposing counsel and, in particular, to their client.

I was the first attorney to arrive on the morning of October 3, 1989, and claimed the trial table closest to the jury box—prime real estate because it allowed us to more easily observe jurors' facial expressions. I plopped my briefcase underneath it and then placed two thin files on its surface. Ben had taught me to keep the surface uncluttered; we wanted the jury to see us as organized and ready. The preferred table secured, I walked out of the courtroom and into the hallway to wait for the clients.

Sitting second chair, I was excited but not nervous. I'd passed the baton to Ben, whose job it was to take the case to the finish line. Along the way, I'd question a few witnesses to give him a breather now and then, and I'd provide feedback when he asked. However, he was the one in the hot seat—the one who'd have to make snap decisions, remain calm when testimony faltered, and be ready to capitalize on the defendants' mistakes. He'd try to connect with the jurors in the jury selection process and start to win them over during his opening statement. As for examinations, he'd be questioning our clients, all the significant lay witnesses, and our three expert witnesses—two doctors and our security expert. He'd need to maintain a high energy level for three to four days, the estimated length of the trial. It was now his case to win or lose.

Marie and Chuck were the next to arrive. Both were dressed conservatively, Chuck in a sport coat and Marie in a suit. Yesterday, Ben had told Marie not to wear any flashy jewelry, which had made her laugh— she didn't own any. I thought about asking Chuck if it felt better sitting in the courtroom as a plaintiff but decided it would be in bad taste to make light of the never-ending asbestos lawsuits.

Ben, Rasmùssen, and Soldat walked into the courtroom around the same time, about ten minutes to nine. The bailiff handed each of us two sheets of paper that contained the names of the prospective jurors, the cities where they resided, and the names of their employers. Some judges required prospective jurors to fill out detailed questionnaires that fleshed out additional background information, but Judge Lawther had not done that.

When the trial began, each side would get the opportunity to question the jurors, find out a little about them, and ask them about particular opinions and experiences that might affect their objectivity in deciding this case. If a prospective juror indicated that he or she could not be fair, the judge would usually excuse them—something called an excuse for cause. Otherwise, each side had three challenges, known as peremptory challenges, with which they could dismiss any juror for any reason. This process was known as jury selection. Ben would go first, followed by the two defense attorneys.

After the jury had been empaneled, each party would give an opening statement. As the plaintiff, we would then begin calling witnesses to establish our case, and when we finished, each defendant would do the same. When all the evidence had been presented, each party would make a closing argument. At the end, the judge would instruct the jury on the law, explain to them the various verdicts they could reach, and direct them to deliberate until they reached a verdict.

There was an order and rhythm to the process—an ancient dance that dated back centuries to English common law. As lawyers we recognized that the jury system had its flaws and missteps, but we believed that in the vast majority of cases, the combined wisdom of those chosen led to a fair result. Pulled from all walks of life, these strangers took their responsibilities seriously and often looked back with pride on their jury service. Unaffected by lobbyists or special-interest groups, the jury would reach a decision that was its alone. The courtroom was the one place where the ordinary citizen had the same standing as a multinational corporation. It was why many of us had become lawyers and why we continued to venerate this age-old institution.

Each trial had its own turning point. Sometimes it was obvious, but at other times, it could only be seen in retrospect. We tried to predict it, but often it came as a complete surprise. In our case, we believed that Marie's testimony and that of Brittany Kirkpatrick would grab the jurors' attention—highlighting the danger that lurked at this restaurant. However, our key witness would be the security expert, Rick Newman, whose testimony would show that those dangers could have been eliminated by implementing some simple and relatively inexpensive solutions—if the owners had actually cared about customer safety.

Our trial theme would follow that same message, namely that the owners just didn't care about customer safety. It would be introduced in our opening statement, developed during testimony, and reinforced in the closing argument. We'd show that the restaurant had taken steps to protect its night deposit and eliminate stealing by employees but hadn't shown the same zeal for protecting its own customers. What had they done after Brittany Kirkpatrick had been abducted by these same two men? Nothing.

The defense would also have a theme, and we had a good idea what it would be. They'd argue that they couldn't control the criminal acts of bad people and shouldn't be expected to. What would happen if every property owner were held responsible for criminal acts that happened on their property? Where would liability stop?

It would be a variation on a common defense theme—"Sorry, bad things happen." Plaintiff lawyers were always surprised by its effectiveness until they looked to social scientists for an answer. Studies showed that our subconscious takes over when we learn of another's catastrophic injuries. Humans instinctively tell themselves that they would have acted differently and avoided the trauma-inducing situation, even when their own past behavior mirrors that of the injured person almost exactly. It is a protective mechanism that makes us feel safer from the "bad things" that befall others. Although it can be overcome, this theme works because it is ingrained in our DNA.

All of our theoretical musings ended when Judge Lawther took the bench at precisely nine o'clock and the trial began. After he confirmed that there were no preliminary matters to discuss, he brought in eighteen prospective jurors. Of the eighteen, twelve were women. None lived in any of the affluent Cuyahoga County suburbs; most resided in Cleveland and the smaller cities that surrounded it. The group included two steelworkers, a schoolteacher, a hospital worker, two real estate brokers, several retail salespeople, miscellaneous office workers, and retired individuals. There were no professionals or high-income occupations among them. All but one were Caucasian.

The majority of the eventual jurors would likely be female, even after each side had excused some of the jurors during the selection process. We had no fixed profile for an ideal juror for Marie's case, but we believed that women would be more sympathetic to her than men.

Based on other social science research, we held several loose opinions about the types of people who were more likely to award large verdicts. Working-class jurors were usually the most generous. They often relished the role of bestowing a large sum of money on a deserving plaintiff. Retired jurors on fixed incomes, and particularly those who had lived through the Depression, often had a difficult time awarding large verdicts. To them, one hundred thousand dollars seemed like a fortune. As a group, upper-middle-class and wealthy jurors were likely to be stingy too. They believed that they had worked hard for their financial well-being (even if they hadn't) and it was fundamentally unfair for others to join them without "earning" it.

Although we would have only a short time to gauge a prospective juror's personality, we favored emotional, outgoing people over detached, analytical types. We also wanted to avoid people who had suffered through injuries and illnesses but had never been compensated for them. If a juror had to live with a disability or chronic condition, they normally were not sympathetic toward plaintiffs who were seeking money for their bad health.

After the bailiff had seated eight prospective jurors in the box, the judge asked them a series of questions that were required by law but weren't likely to apply to any of them. For example, did they have a case pending against any of the parties? Were they going to be called as witnesses in this case? After finishing these questions, the judge turned the selection process over to Ben.

Ben introduced himself, the clients, and me and had us stand. Before he asked specific questions to the prospective jurors, he explained why each attorney would be questioning them.

"We each come into this courtroom with our own beliefs and experiences. Each side is entitled to jurors who will be fair and impartial. We'll be asking questions about you, not to pry, but to find out if there is any reason why you might not be right for this case. The system works only if all the parties start at the same place. No one is entitled to a head start or a juror who favors one side over the other before he or she has heard any evidence. Does that make sense to you? If so, please raise your hands."

All eight raised their hands, some nodding as they did so.

For the next few minutes, Ben began by outlining the stages of the trial. Most had never served on a jury before and found it reassuring to learn the order of things and to understand their role in the proceedings. When an attorney provided this information, the jurors began to view him or her with trust. He next explained a little about the case and asked if knowing those few facts would cause any of them to favor one side over the other. No one raised a hand.

"This is a civil case, and the burden of proof is upon our side, the plaintiff, to prove its case by a preponderance of the evidence. How many of you have heard that phrase, 'preponderance of the evidence'?"

One juror raised her hand.

"Ms. Sauer, you raised your hand. Do you know what that means?"

"No, I've just heard those words, that's all."

"Well, it means the greater weight of the evidence. It's a different standard than in a criminal case, where the prosecutor has to prove the case beyond a reasonable doubt. 'Preponderance of the evidence' means—well—fifty-one percent. If we put the plaintiff's evidence on one side of the scale of justice and the defendant's on the other side, the plaintiff's evidence has to tip the scale ever so slightly downward. The plaintiff's evidence must outweigh the evidence opposed to it in order to establish its case. Do you understand that, Ms. Sauer?"

She nodded.

"How about the rest of you? Will you agree that you'll decide the case based on the greater weight of the evidence and not by proof beyond a reasonable doubt? If so, please raise your hands."

All eight raised their hands. They also agreed that if we proved our case by a preponderance of the evidence, they would rule in our favor.

Ben then turned the question around. "And if we fail to prove our case by a preponderance of the evidence, your duty will be to find for the defendants. That's what the law requires you to do. Will you do that?" By phrasing the question from the defendants' viewpoint, he looked fair-minded. Whatever happened, we could live with the consequences. Expecting no favors, he exuded a subtle confidence.

Again, they agreed.

Ben talked to each juror individually. He inquired about their jobs, families, prior jury experience, and prior lawsuits. He inquired about their hobbies, their social memberships, and their thoughts about the civil justice system. He wanted to establish a dialogue with each one. In this exchange, we were trying to glimpse who each juror was—not just their personality type but whether they had any hint of hostility toward our case.

After Ben sat down, John Rasmussen took his place. He explained that Ben had asked many of the questions that were important to him, and he wouldn't repeat them. He did ask them to reserve any conclusions about fault until they'd heard all of the evidence, both the plaintiff's and the defendants'. He talked about sympathy and how it could influence decision-making. Could the jurors base their decision on the facts and the law and not sympathy? They uniformly agreed that they could.

"I want to go a bit farther than Mr. Barrett and give you the names of all the witnesses that will testify in this case just to make sure that none of you know them." He listed all of the doctors who had treated Marie and every fact witness who would testify about the occurrence. None of the jurors knew any of these witnesses.

"Mrs. Grossman was on her way to Hawken School to watch her son wrestle that evening. Do any of you have children that attend Hawken School or family members who work at that school?"

It was a legitimate question; however, he was informing the jurors at the outset that Marie and Chuck could afford to send their children to a private school. It separated our clients from the prospective jurors who were without the financial resources to do the same.

"Mrs. Grossman has worked as an attorney for the law firm of Jones Day and later in the legal department of the bank AmeriTrust. Have any of you or any of your immediate family members worked there?"

One woman raised her hand and told him that she had once been employed as a teller at the bank but did not know Mrs. Grossman. Rasmussen asked a similar question about Chuck's company and whether any of the panel's family members had ever worked there. None had.

Frank Soldat was the last attorney to address the prospective jurors. In keeping with his decision to maintain a low profile, he asked just a few questions. He wanted to know if any of the panel had ever had a bad experience at Burger King. Some of the jurors smiled, but no one complained about the quality of their food or any other unpleasant restaurant experience.

"Burger King Corporation, my client, owns some of the Burger King restaurants, but most are owned by other companies called franchisees. This restaurant was run by a franchisee, and my client had no control over its operation. Do you understand that there has to be some—"

"Objection," Ben said. "This sounds like an argument and not a question."

"Sustained," Judge Lawther said. "This is jury selection, Mr. Soldat. Do you have a question for a juror somewhere in there?"

"I was just getting to that, Your Honor," Soldat replied as he noisily flipped through several pages on his yellow pad. "Will any of you just award damages to Mrs. Grossman because she was hurt on the Burger King property, or will you require the plaintiff to prove that we were negligent?"

Each juror confirmed that they would require proof of negligence, and Soldat sat down.

Ben and I reviewed the prospective-jurors list. We both had reservations about Juror Number Three. After Ben had asked her if she thought businesses had an obligation to make their property safe for customers, she had looked away before saying, "I suppose so." She'd also shown little or no emotion when answering his questions but had been decidedly more pleasant when Rasmussen had examined her.

"Mr. Barrett, will you exercise a peremptory challenge?" Judge Lawther asked.

"Yes, Your Honor, we will. We would excuse and thank Juror Number Three."

"Juror Number Three, Ms. Handshaw, you are excused. Juror Number Nine, Ms. Malich, please take Ms. Handshaw's seat."

After the new prospective juror was seated, Ben and later the two defense attorneys questioned her in the same manner as they had done previously. It was a laborious process, and it soon was time for the noon recess. A few minutes after twelve, the judge told the prospective jurors that we would adjourn for lunch and that they should return to the jury room by 1:15.

After lunch, the two defense attorneys excused Juror Number One. Although both of them had requested three peremptory challenges each, Judge Lawther had refused, claiming that their interests were similar and that they would share three challenges. As a result, they'd needed to talk between themselves and agree on the person to be excused.

The process continued well into the afternoon as each side continued to excuse jurors and interview their replacements. By the time of the midafternoon recess, eight jurors had been selected, along with one alternate juror who would replace one of the regular jurors in case of illness or some other incapacity.

At the break, Marie asked me what I thought of the jury. She'd been a keen observer throughout the selection process, listening not just to their answers but also to the discussions Ben and I had as we debated which jurors to dismiss. I smiled. "It seems like a good panel," I said. "They seem to be a good cross-section of working-class and middle-class America. No one seems to have any strong beliefs that could work against us. I think they'll be fair."

"I like that there are five women on the jury," Marie said. "I think they'll understand how vulnerable I was that evening and why I did what I did."

I nodded in agreement. I thought that, too, but also knew that women jurors could sometimes be more critical of women plaintiffs than men were.

When court resumed at 3 p.m., the judge told the jurors that they would hear opening statements from each attorney. Judge Lawther explained that an opening statement was a preview of the case, a framework that laid out what each side expected to prove. The attorneys' statements were not evidence, and they were to limit their presentations to the facts of the case and not venture into conclusions or resort to argument.

The opening statement was a crucial part of our case. Studies showed that if jurors agreed with your position after the opening statement, they'd almost always rule the same way at the end of the case. Some studies put the likelihood at 80 percent. A psychological phenomenon known as primacy was responsible for this tendency. For some reason, a person's first impressions carried more weight than contrary evidence learned at a later time. Ben's opening statement needed to harness the power of primacy.

Because the boundary between fact and argument was sometimes murky, attorneys usually crossed it several times during their opening statements. However, if the trespass was brief, normally no one objected. Attorneys hated to be interrupted during an opening statement or closing argument because it stopped their momentum. Mindful of that, we usually let our opponents have some leeway in their presentations, expecting the favor to be returned when it was our turn to address the jury.

Ben began his opening statement by telling the jury about Marie, first her background and then why she'd stopped at the Burger King that evening. He stood without notes about five to six feet from the jury box rail—close, but not so close as to invade their space. His voice was quiet and calm, almost conversational. I glanced at Marie, who was staring at the jury. Like me, she wanted to study their reactions as Ben told them about the events of December 11, 1987.

Although they had spent most of the day in the courtroom, the jurors were still attentive. For the most part, their eyes stayed fixed on Ben, occasionally glancing at Marie. Their faces, however, remained impassive and unreadable, even after Ben became more animated and told them that Marie had been shot in the head. No one winced. No one looked away. No one shook their head in disbelief.

The only person who showed any emotion was Judge Lawther. He shuddered. The judge maintained a pained expression as Ben told the jury how Marie had staggered from her car, held her bleeding and dislocated jaw in one hand, and dashed into the restaurant. For a moment, the judge stared at Marie as if searching for signs of the bullet hole. He made eye contact with the bailiff and raised his eyebrows.

How would the jury react when they learned that the same two men had abducted another woman six weeks earlier and Burger King had done nothing to increase security? Upon learning this, two women jurors shook their heads and scowled toward the defense table, where Rasmussen and Soldat sat with corporate representatives. Harold Stillwater had opted not to attend the trial and had instead sent his fiscal officer, Neil Sommers, in his place. Burger King's designee, Jack Artman, sat next to him in a gray suit, tapping a pen against the back of his left hand. Both men instinctively looked down when the two women shot them disapproving looks.

"The defendants had experienced crimes involving guns at this location for years. You'll learn that over the past seven years, twelve crimes had been committed there involving guns to both customers and employees, yet the defendants did nothing. They just turned a blind eye."

I looked over at John Rasmussen, expecting him to object because Ben had crossed the line between reciting facts and journeying into argument. Rasmussen began to stand, but then sat down as Ben began previewing the security expert's findings.

Ben's voice and demeanor had changed again. He was now indignant as he outlined the simple measures that our security expert believed were essential for this location and had never been implemented. After criticizing the restaurant for its limited use of security guards and failure to provide outdoor video surveillance, Ben took issue with the restaurant's layout.

"Mr. Newman will tell you that the restaurant should also have constructed a fence around its parking lot to limit access. It's a simple step that has been proven to discourage criminal activity. That's exactly what the Cleveland Play House did across the street from this Burger King. Its parking lot is surrounded by a tall, decorative black fence."

One male juror nodded. The others maintained neutral expressions, but they seemed focused and engaged. I was encouraged that none sat with arms folded in front of them, the universal sign that one's message was being rejected.

Ben returned to his conversational tone as he summarized Marie's injuries and treatment. "Marie will be the first to tell you that she is very fortunate to be alive. If the bullet had entered several inches higher, she would have died instantly. You'll learn that Marie is a very determined woman, and she used her strong will to do everything in her power to recover."

As Ben described her surgeries and treatment, the jurors switched their focus back and forth between him and Marie. They seemed interested in learning and understanding the full extent of her injuries.

Ben continued, "Despite the best of care at the Cleveland Clinic, Marie will never return to the person she was before this incident. The bullet destroyed nerves—nerves that control feeling in her chin and lip. She can't sense if there is food on her chin. As for her sense of taste—well, it's almost completely gone. She can't open her jaw wide enough to bite into an apple or a thick sandwich. As for speech, she no longer can speak as clearly or as quickly as she did before these injuries. As an attorney and businesswoman, this is a terrible drawback.

"You'll learn more about this from Marie and from her surgeon, Dr. Zins. These changes are permanent. That means that they'll never get better.

"Besides the physical injuries, there will always be emotional trauma. Marie relives the shooting every day. It will always haunt her."

Ben concluded by telling the jury that this event and these injuries were very avoidable. "If the defendants had really cared about customer safety, they could have made simple improvements years ago. They never did, and this is the result. It will be your job to hold them accountable."

John Rasmussen walked slowly to the spot where Ben had been standing just moments before. His job was to recover the ground his side had lost during Ben's opening. He looked composed and confident. Turning toward Marie, he told the jury that everyone, his client especially, wished that Mrs. Grossman had never been injured at this Burger King.

"She's an amazing woman. She certainly has our sympathy for what happened to her on December 11, 1987. She also has our respect for all that she has endured and accomplished since the shooting. As awful as all of that was, the question remains whether her injuries were *caused* by the restaurant's negligence. Did my client *cause* her injuries? Please remember that there are always two sides to a story and here are the facts as we see them."

Rasmussen had the jury's attention, and I was impressed by the way he'd captured it. He'd expressed sympathy for the plaintiff, something the jurors no doubt felt. He'd emphasized the word "cause" twice at the very beginning of his opening statement. The immediate "cause" of Marie's injuries was the action of a criminal, not the supposed failings of the restaurant. It was a way to focus the jury's attention on the real culprits.

He next wanted to humanize his client. He explained that Harold Stillwater was a former marine who had started his businesses more than twenty years ago with virtually nothing. At his core, he was a man who cared about people and his community. He'd taken over the struggling Burger King at East Eighty-Fifth and Euclid from another owner and gambled that he could make it work. He'd wanted to offer employment to the neighborhood residents, show confidence in the area, and provide an economic engine that would encourage others businesses to invest there.

"This restaurant is located on the border of the Hough neighborhood. As most of us remember, in 1966, Hough had riots that resulted in several deaths and caused millions of dollars of damage before the police and National Guard restored order. Most of its residents are peaceful, law-abiding people; however, it has some of the highest crime rates in the city. The easy thing would have been for Mr. Stillwater to give up on this restaurant and the people who live in Hough, but he didn't."

Rasmussen explained that his client had taken measures to keep the premises safe. The lighting in the parking lot was bright. He'd hired a security guard who came each night at 7:30 p.m. and stayed until 9:30 p.m., a period that they considered the most vulnerable for customers and employees. The restaurant often went months without any criminal activity at all. Although any incident was unfortunate, this location averaged only one or two a year.

"We would ask you to hold the plaintiff to her burden of proof. She will have to demonstrate that if we had taken all of the measures that her expert recommends, this incident would not have happened. Unfortunately, crimes happen swiftly and without warning. Crimes occur even when security guards are present and when video surveillance cameras are in place. It all sounds great in theory, but that's not the real world. You can't always prevent a crime from occurring in a parking lot, especially in Hough. You shouldn't be expected to, and that's not what the law requires us to do. We are required to take reasonable precautions, and that's exactly what we did. I'm confident that after you have heard all of the evidence, you will return a verdict in favor of the defendants, Harold Stillwater and Quick Eats Enterprises. Thank you."

Frank Soldat gave one of the shortest opening statements that I had ever witnessed. He explained that Burger King had two types of restaurants: those owned by Burger King itself and those that were run by franchisees. This restaurant was owned by a franchisee.

"We simply had no say on how this restaurant was run. We did not set the guidelines for security nor take an active part in any of its operations. None of our employees worked there, and none were negligent."

He closed by asking the jury to render a verdict in favor of Burger King at the end of the case.

Soldat finished his brief statement just after 4 p.m. Judge Lawther dismissed the jury and told them to report to the jury room at 8:45 the next day.

As we gathered our papers, Chuck asked us what we thought so far. I could tell that Ben was exhausted so I fielded the question. "We seem to have a fair jury—working-class and middle-class people. They were attentive to both sides during their opening statements."

Chuck nodded, but his expression hinted that he wanted more reassurance.

Sensing this, Ben added, "I'm encouraged. As they say, so far, so good. Ask me tomorrow after some of our witnesses have testified. Remember, there will always be ups and downs in a trial, but it was a good first day."

19

DAY TWO

We would begin the second day of the trial by calling witnesses who would tell the jurors what happened on the evening of December 11, 1987. In the course of this testimony, we would extract the evidence that would establish the defendants' liability. Jurors didn't want to hear about your client's injuries until you'd established the other party's fault. Until then, evidence of injuries was premature and presumptuous. Even though Marie was our strongest witness, her testimony would have to wait.

Detective Nowak was the first witness to take the stand. Although a frequent participant in criminal trials, this would be the first time he'd recount a criminal investigation to a civil jury. At ease in the witness chair, he told the jury how the police had apprehended Richard Thompson and Christopher Martin. I could hear the pride in his voice as he told of their quick arrest, conviction, and ultimate imprisonment. Detective Nowak explained that these same two men had also abducted and robbed another woman, Brittany Kirkpatrick, from this same drive-thru six weeks earlier. After establishing that he had been involved in the earlier investigation, Ben asked him if he had noticed any changes at the Burger King property after the first incident. He hadn't.

"Did you talk with Marie Grossman on the night of the shooting?" Ben asked.

"I asked questions, and she wrote answers on a pad of paper. She'd just come out of surgery, but she was still—I'm not sure of the right words here—she was really hyper."

"What did she look like?"

"Oh, not so good. The whole left side of her face was really swollen and badly discolored. She was bandaged. I've seen worse in my job, but hers was pretty bad. I mean—she'd just taken a bullet to her head at close range and survived. She was very lucky to be alive, and she knew it." The detective looked over at Marie before he continued. "She looks a heck of a lot better today than she did two years ago—I can tell you that."

"Did she help in your investigation?"

"I came back the next day, and she identified her shooter from a group of photos. When she got out of the hospital, she came to the preliminary hearing and pointed him out, even though she had a tracheotomy tube and couldn't talk. She was a real trooper."

On cross-examination, Rasmussen established that Nowak worked in the Fifth District, which included Hough and Fairfax. He admitted that these were two of the highest-crime areas in the city and businesses were frequently robbed at gunpoint. The Cleveland Clinic was located nearby, and to reduce crime against its employees and patients, it employed a security force that was the second largest in Cuyahoga County.

Patrolman Hupka replaced Nowak on the stand. He'd been the first to arrive at the scene and had located two eyewitnesses to the shooting, two women whom we'd also subpoenaed to testify as part of our case. We'd asked Patrolman Hupka to bring photographs of the crime scene, and he identified them for the jury. When the jurors deliberated, they would see exactly what the restaurant looked like that evening. They'd see photos of the menu board, the parking lot (with one of the assailants' cars still there), and the interior of the restaurant, where several photographs captured Marie's blood on the floor and front counter.

"This photograph of the back of the Burger King, is this a fair and accurate representation of what the restaurant looked like on December 11, 1987?" Ben asked.

"Yes. All of these photographs were taken either that night or the next day."

"I see that there are no windows on the back of the building and no window on the back door. Is that correct?"

The police officer picked up the photograph and studied it for a moment before answering. "No windows anywhere in the back."

"No way for employees to see what is going on in the back parking lot, is there?"

"Not unless they opened the back door and took a look out," he replied.

"Do you see any video surveillance cameras mounted on the building?"

This time the officer squinted as he searched the photograph. "I don't think so," he replied.

Neither defense attorney questioned him.

Although we only needed one of the eyewitnesses to testify, I had subpoenaed both of them in case one failed to show. After the midday break, we decided to call both of them because they had both made sacrifices to be in court. Fortunately, their testimony was consistent and powerful. They told the jury that for well over an hour, they'd watched these men loitering about the parking lot, sometimes inside a car and other times wandering about the lot. They'd seen the tall man approach the blue Mustang and stick a gun through the open driver's window, and then heard the gun's report as the car moved forward.

"During this hour to an hour and a half when these men were loitering in the Burger King parking lot, did you ever see any employee from Burger King approach them?" Ben asked Sheila Williams.

"Not that I saw, but I wasn't looking out the window the entire time," she said.

"How often did you leave the window?"

"We never left the window. We were sitting in chairs in front of the window, talking—you know—Christy and me. So we looked at each other while we talked, but we was also looking outside too. That's how we knew that each of the guys had a car there. We'd seen them in two different cars from time to time."

Before the noon break, Officer Philip Meli took the stand. He had not been involved in the Burger King investigation, but we'd asked him to bring the crime statistics for the area surrounding the restaurant. Our expert's opinions would be based partly upon the level of crime in the area, and we needed to get that into evidence. Before we excused him, the officer identified the documents and briefly explained them. His testimony concluded the morning session. In the afternoon, we planned to call individuals who worked either at the restaurant or for the franchisee.

Immediately after eating lunch, jurors rarely are alert. Several struggle to keep awake, and it's not unusual to see one actually napping. Of the four people we had slated to testify in the afternoon, only one was likely to command the jury's attention. She was Mylayna Albright, the soft-spoken young woman who had taken Marie's order that night. However, she was not going to testify live. Her testimony had been prerecorded on videotape a week before and would be played to the jury. Videotaped testimony never packs the same punch as a live witness, but we decided to play her testimony first.

I had subpoenaed all of our witnesses two weeks before the trial. A few days later, Rasmussen had phoned to let me know that Albright's family had contacted him, advising that Mylayna was a student at Ohio State University in Columbus. Although the subpoena had been left at her house in Cleveland, she had not been personally served and was under no obligation to attend. Some attorneys in Rasmussen's position would have kept this knowledge to themselves and watched us scramble at trial when she did not show up. Fortunately for us, Rasmussen followed a higher code and had called me. We'd made arrangements to videotape her testimony in Columbus at the Ohio State Bar Association office, located on the periphery of the campus. A week before trial, Rasmussen, Soldat, and I had driven to Columbus to take a deposition that lasted all of thirty minutes.

The bailiff wheeled in a television set on a cart and positioned it in front of the jury. After the judge explained what was happening, the video recorder was turned on and Albright appeared on the screen with her right hand raised as she took the oath. Her testimony mirrored what she'd told me during her deposition six months earlier. It had been a quiet Friday evening when Mrs. Grossman pulled up to the menu board around 6:20. She'd placed her order, which was followed by silence and then the report of the gunshot.

She seemed more confident than she had during her earlier deposition. Her voice, captured by a clip-on microphone, was loud and clear. As she had done previously, she became visibly upset when she recounted Marie's appearance after she entered the restaurant. However, this was not the reason we had gone to such trouble to preserve her testimony. We wanted the jury to learn that she had quit her job because she'd feared for her safety when she arrived in the early morning darkness without a security guard present.

During the videotaping, both defense attorneys had objected when I'd asked these questions, claiming they were irrelevant. The witness had answered, but her videotaped responses would only be played to the jury if the judge later ruled that her testimony was admissible. He'd ruled in our favor, and the videotape was played without interruption.

Through this witness, we also established that the restaurant's only video camera was directed at employees working the counter, presumably to discourage stealing. According to Mylayna, security guards remained primarily inside the restaurant during the few hours they worked there. From her observations, they did not regularly patrol the parking lot unless they were first informed of a disturbance. Again, she remembered that after closing, the guards escorted the assistant manager to his car before he drove away to make the night deposit.

Our expert had criticized the restaurant because it had not trained its employees to be aware of suspicious behavior, including loitering. She confirmed that she had not received that type of training.

When Rasmussen questioned her, she admitted that she had never been approached or accosted by anyone when she arrived for her early morning shift. When pressed, she also expressed uncertainty about the security guards' minute-by-minute activities, leaving open the possibility that they did monitor outside activity on a more regular basis.

After Mylayna Albright's testimony concluded, we called the franchisee's comptroller, Neil Sommers, to the stand. I'd taken his deposition earlier, and he'd come across as a straight shooter whose principal role was to handle the money issues associated with the business. He had no role in the actual operation of the individual restaurants; however, he gathered and maintained all of the incident reports associated with their string of Burger Kings. Through him, we laid a foundation for the admission of the incident reports. We now could compare the frequency of criminal activity at the Burger King in question to the others that they owned.

After a longer-than-expected midafternoon break, we called Ronald Stillwater to the stand. It was 3 p.m., and he would likely be the day's last witness. We explained to the court that we were calling Mr. Stillwater as if upon cross-examination.

I'd deposed Stillwater several months before and had found him to be a feisty witness. I knew that Ben would try to control him by asking short, leading questions that Stillwater would have to answer with either a yes or a no.

When Stillwater entered the courtroom, I was reminded how tall and imposing a figure he cut. He was dressed in a navy-blue suit that gave him a look of authority. The arrogance I had witnessed several months earlier was gone, replaced by a thoughtful and polite manner. Rasmussen had obviously worked with him in preparation for his testimony.

As Ben ran through his questions, the younger Stillwater answered them without the gratuitous comments that had peppered his earlier testimony. He conceded that the company did not train its employees to be on the alert for suspicious behavior. They did not have video surveillance cameras that monitored outside activities. Their security guards worked for two hours every night. He admitted that he had become aware of the earlier incident involving Brittany Kirkpatrick.

"After you learned about it, you did not add video surveillance to your parking lot?"

"We considered that."

"That wasn't my question. Did you add it?"

"No."

"After this earlier incident, did you increase security guard coverage to include coverage whenever it was dark outside?"

"We were kicking around some ideas about this, but no, we did not implement that."

"Did you increase security guard coverage at all?"

"No." Although he'd kept his answer short, he looked frustrated.

"Did you have anyone in the security field come out and provide you with an analysis and plan for improvements?"

"No, we didn't," he said, blowing his breath upward and scowling for the first time.

"You didn't construct a fence around the parking lot's perimeter, did you?"

"No, we didn't."

"Wouldn't a fence and a controlled access make your property safer? They'd done that across the street at the Cleveland Play House parking lot."

"Yes, it might have."

"But you didn't consider this?"

"Yes, we did consider it," Stillwater said, his voice agitated for the first time. "I went down to city hall and to the building department and filled out the paperwork to get the process started."

Now it was Ben who was reeling, and Stillwater sensed it. Even though no question was posed, Stillwater continued. "I went down there, and the application for a fence got killed in red tape. We were going to have to appeal something, and we just couldn't do this in six weeks."

Ben walked over to our trial table and calmly picked up Stillwater's deposition transcript. He flipped through a few pages and found what he was looking for.

"Mr. Stillwater, do you remember my partner taking your deposition on February 13, 1989?"

"I don't remember the exact date, but I remember my deposition several months ago."

"Do you remember being under oath at this time?"

"Yes, of course, I was."

Ben handed an extra copy of the deposition to Stillwater. "At page thirty-two of your deposition, you were asked if you had considered making any security changes after the earlier abduction at the drive-thru. Your answer was 'We were pricing out video cameras. We were thinking about increasing the hours for our security guards.' Then you were asked, 'But none of those changes had been accomplished?' And you answer was 'Right.' Were those the questions and answers that were posed to you then?"

"Yes."

"You made no mention of constructing a fence, nor did you say anything about your difficulties at the Cleveland building department?"

"It slipped my mind at the time, but I definitely made an effort. I just got zero help from the Cleveland bureaucracy."

On that unsatisfactory note, Ben concluded his cross-examination. While the judge dismissed the jury for the day, I pulled a large expandable file from under our trial table and searched for the Cleveland building department records that I'd obtained before the case had been filed. As Ben was loading his file into his briefcase, I found it. I quickly looked through the forty or so pages and saw no paperwork about a fence.

"I've got the building department file, and there's no application for a fence in it," I told Ben.

"Really. Let me see it." He rifled through it and then looked at his watch. "Who'd you talk to there?"

"I don't know; that was a year and a half ago," I said. I grabbed the file back and opened it again. After the employee had copied the records, I'd paid him and he'd given me a receipt. I spotted the hand-written receipt, crumpled between two pages. "His name is Tony Constanzo."

"We're going to talk to him right now and perhaps put him on the stand first thing tomorrow," he said. "It's only 4 p.m. He's probably still there for a half an hour, and it's only a block away."

"He's not on our witness list," I said, wondering if all this would be in vain when the defense objected to his testimony and the judge confirmed that we had not identified him as a witness.

"I don't care," Ben snapped. "I'm not going to worry about that now. Let's see if this guy can help us first."

Ten minutes later, we were at the Cleveland city hall and inside the building department office.

"That's the guy," I said, pointing toward Anthony Constanzo.

Ben grabbed Constanzo's attention, and he walked to the counter to talk to us. Ben quickly told him what had happened in the courtroom minutes earlier.

"The owner's son claimed that the building department had halted his plan to construct a fence around the restaurant's parking lot. He said someone denied his application. You copied the file for us months ago, and there was no record of this in the stuff you gave us."

"Let me pull my file," he said. For the next five minutes, Constanzo leafed through his file. Finally, he looked up. "There's no application for a fence in here."

"Do you keep records of conversations in the file?" Ben asked.

"We do. I'm the guy he would've talked to. I even keep little summaries of phone conversations. This guy never came in here or talked to me."

"Will you testify to that tomorrow at 9 a.m.?" Ben asked.

"You got a subpoena for me? I gotta show one to my boss, you know."

"What time do you start in the morning?" Ben asked.

"Eight o'clock."

"We'll get a subpoena for you first thing when the clerk's office opens tomorrow at 8 a.m., and David will run it over to you around 8:20. You'll have your subpoena. Can you let your boss know now that you'll be gone for about a half an hour tomorrow?"

"Sure. I'll tell him if he hasn't already left. Don't worry; as long as you get me that subpoena, I'll be there."

"And you bring a complete copy of your file along with the original. Okay?" Ben confirmed.

"I'll do that," Constanzo said. "Hey, I think I'll enjoy this little break from the old routine."

As we walked back to our cars, I was still concerned that the judge wouldn't allow the building department employee to testify tomorrow. The civil rules and the local court rules did not allow surprise witnesses.

Ben was undaunted. "Look, Stillwater surprised us with testimony that's inconsistent with his deposition. The defense opened the door here, and they can't complain when we challenge this."

"Opening the door" was a loose evidentiary rule that allowed one party to counter the other's evidence after the other side had introduced a topic. This was true even when the counter-evidence would initially have been excluded because of some evidentiary prohibition. After opening the door, the other side could no longer protest when more evidence was introduced on the same subject.

"Yeah, I think you're right," I said.

"I know I'm right," Ben said.

20

DAY THREE

Before the third day's proceedings began, Ben walked over to the defense table and told both attorneys that we were calling a building department employee to contradict Ron Stillwater's testimony. Neither Rasmussen nor Soldat uttered a word in protest. Earlier that morning, I'd delivered the subpoena to Anthony Constanzo, and he'd decided to walk to the courthouse with me and sit outside the courtroom until he was called.

He was neatly dressed in a brown plaid sport coat, a tie, and tan pants. He clutched his file to his chest as he walked through the courtroom and took his seat in the witness chair. Constanzo told the jury that he'd been employed by the city of Cleveland for over a decade. He explained that at the building department, the city maintained a file on every commercial property. He'd brought the one involving the Burger King restaurant located at East Eighty-Fifth and Euclid Avenue and confirmed that he had reviewed it yesterday and again today.

"Mr. Constanzo, is there any paperwork in your file that shows that the owners of this restaurant applied to the city to construct a fence at any time?"

"No, sir, there is not," he replied.

"Well, just to be sure that you did not overlook anything, would you please identify every document in your file and tell the jury what it is?"

For the next ten minutes, Constanzo did just that, painstakingly explaining to the jurors every document, just as he had done with me over a year ago. When he'd finished, the jury knew that his file contained nothing that even remotely referenced a proposed fence.

"I want you to be very complete. Is it possible that there is a phone conversation that you had with the restaurant owners?"

"I keep summaries of all phone conversations in the file. There isn't one about a fence."

"What about unofficial notes?"

"Yeah, I write down notes if someone comes in and we discuss something. Nothing like that about a fence."

Ben concluded his questioning, and neither defense attorney cross-examined the witness. I was particularly interested in Rasmussen's reaction, but his face betrayed no emotion.

It was now up to the jury to evaluate this development. It was possible that Stillwater had actually spoken with someone in the building department and nothing had been recorded about it. However, he'd talked about paperwork, and there was none in the file. This would be a difficult thing for his attorney to explain away. We hoped that the jurors would conclude that he'd invented the story to make the restaurant seem more concerned and responsive to crime than it actually had been. The jury would eventually tell us which scenario seemed more likely.

Ben told the court that the plaintiff was calling Jack Artman to the stand as if upon cross-examination. Artman was the Burger King representative in Northeast Ohio who monitored the restaurants there. When I'd deposed him, he'd maintained that neither he nor Burger King had any control over the franchisees in the day-to-day operations of their restaurants. However, he'd admitted that Burger King required the franchisees to follow an operations manual that dictated many standards for the restaurant. Throughout the deposition, he'd insisted that he'd never given any directives to Stillwater or any of his management team.

Taking a seat in the witness chair, Artman moved about, apparently unable to find a comfortable position. After he was seated, he smiled at the jury, but his expression quickly degenerated into a grimace. Ben's first questions established his employment with Burger King and that he inspected area Burger King restaurants as part of his duties.

Picking up the operations manual, Ben began by confirming that a franchisee was expected to operate its restaurant pursuant to the manual. Ben ticked off the things that were controlled by the manual, some big and others minute. When he was through, Artman had agreed that the manual set forth the layout of the building, the location for the drive-thru, the foods to be served and their cost, the temperature of the hamburgers, the design of the employees' uniforms, and the standards for restaurant cleanliness.

"These are just a few examples of the standards, right?" Ben asked.

"Yes, the manual covers many topics," Artman replied.

"If one restaurant didn't follow the standards, it would impact the reputation of the entire operation, wouldn't it?"

"It depends on which standard," Artman replied.

"Well, if the parking lot was a mess with potholes and trash strewn about, that's something that would negatively impact the Burger King reputation, would you agree?"

"For the customers who saw it, I suppose," Artman said.

"I mean, you go in unannounced to restaurants, eat the sandwiches, judge the efficiency of their employees, check out the restaurants, don't you?"

"Yes, I do."

"You've visited the Burger King at 8515 Euclid and inspected it, haven't you?"

"Yes."

"If you're not pleased with some aspect of the restaurant's operation because it does not meet the standards of the manual, you will tell the owners, right?"

"Yes, of course."

"And the owners are supposed to correct those problems?"

"Yes."

"And if they don't, Burger King can pull the franchise—in other words, shut them down—right?"

"I've never seen anything that came close to that—ever."

"I'm not asking you about what you've witnessed. I'm asking if Burger King can close down a franchisee's restaurant for failure to follow the Burger King standards."

"Well, it would have to be some very serious violations," Artman replied.

"It's in the franchise agreement, isn't it, that Burger King has a right to revoke a franchise if the owners don't operate the restaurant according to your standards as set in your manual? Right?"

"In theory, yes, but I've never seen it happen."

"But when you tell a franchisee to make some changes, they listen to you because Burger King has clout; they can yank the franchise, is that correct?"

"They listen because they want to be in compliance," Artman protested.

"If they don't listen, they're not in compliance and Burger King can take steps to revoke their franchise. Correct?"

"Yes, but it never happens."

"But it can revoke a franchise. Isn't that true?"

"Yes."

The witness had agreed that Burger King could exercise control by revoking a franchise. I thought Ben would stop his cross-examination at this point, but he continued, apparently wanting the answer wrapped in a big blue ribbon.

"In this sense—with your ability to revoke a franchise for failure to comply with Burger King standards—you have a way to control the franchisee, don't you?"

"Yes."

"A right to control them?"

"Yes."

I looked over at Frank Soldat, who flipped his pen onto his legal pad. His eyes bulged in exasperation. Obviously, he believed that his witness had stumbled into a damning admission. Under the law, Burger King would be liable for the acts of its franchisee if it maintained a right to control it. If we could prove negligence on the part of its franchisee, Burger King would now be liable for that negligence too.

I didn't believe that Artman had said anything that wasn't patently obvious from reading the franchise agreement. When cornered, he'd simply told the truth.

The judge announced the midmorning recess, and during the break, we huddled a moment with Marie, who would be our next witness. Stealing a glance at the defense table, I saw Soldat speaking animatedly with Artman. I looked for Rasmussen, but he'd apparently left the courtroom.

For the remainder of the morning, first Ben and then the defense attorneys questioned Marie. As I'd expected, she was poised and thoughtful with her responses. Because I was familiar with the event, her injuries, and her treatment, I did not concentrate on Marie but instead focused on the jurors' reactions to her testimony. I could see that she held their attention throughout, but none winced or shook their heads in disbelief during the more graphic parts of her story. This was usually the case with jurors—they held their cards close to their vests until a verdict was announced in open court. Only then did you know if you had swayed them.

Both defense attorneys were careful with their questions. If they came across as heavy-handed, the jurors would not like this. Instead, they were polite and gentle during their questioning, focusing more on her recovery than anything else. They were trying to minimize her damages, and this was a safe way to do it. Not ready to abandon the defense of comparative negligence, Rasmussen did ask a few questions about her decision to press down on the accelerator when a gun was pointed at her head. She again stopped him by explaining that she'd feared that she would be raped and killed if she let the men into the car. She told him that she had no choice after she'd offered them her purse and the keys to her car. A woman juror nodded in agreement. As far as I was concerned, this defense would backfire on him if he argued it during his closing.

We broke late for lunch, leaving the courtroom around 12:30. Our expert, Rick Newman, had arrived the night before from Houston. Staying at a downtown hotel, he'd wanted to inspect the Burger King restaurant one last time that morning. Brad Clark, who'd gone with me months before to check out the Burger King, was picking him up at the hotel and driving him to the site before bringing him to the courthouse. We spotted him in the hallway as we were leaving, and he joined us for lunch. We brought him up to date about the trial. Before we headed back, Ben and he discussed the five criticisms Newman had leveled against the restaurant for its security lapses.

When we walked into the courtroom, Judge Lawther was leaning against the jury box rail. He beckoned Ben and me to him.

"I've been approached by both defense attorneys, who have expressed an interest in settling the case. They want to know if your demand for settlement is still the same figure that you expressed several days ago at our pretrial conference."

Ben and I exchanged glances. We'd talked to Marie and Chuck about that settlement demand before the final meeting with the judge three days ago, and they had agreed with our recommendation then.

"I suppose it is," Ben said. "What's their offer?"

"If your demand is the same, the case is settled. Both defense attorneys have been on the phone with their adjusters—off and on all morning and during the lunch recess. They have the money to settle the case with you."

"Okay. We'll talk to our clients," Ben said.

"I'll delay the start of the afternoon session as we work this out," Judge Lawther said.

As we walked away, Ben said to me, "I hate this. I'm in the middle of trial, and now they want to settle."

"They're offering to pay our demand; that's a first," I said. Insurance companies rarely, if ever, agreed to do this; they always countered with a lower figure. Liberty Mutual obviously wanted to end this case right now.

One of the most difficult things for any trial lawyer to do is to switch gears from waging war to suing for peace. These actions require diametrically opposed mind-sets. In one, we are out to destroy and conquer, while in the other, we are measured and diplomatic. Some attorneys will cut off all settlement discussions a week before trial because negotiations become such a distraction, funneling needed energy away from trial preparation. In Marie's case, we were heading into the home stretch with much of the hard work already behind us. The trial was going well, and we wanted to know what a jury would ultimately do with our case.

Marie and Chuck were seated at our trial table as we approached them. Marie seemed relaxed and relieved now that her testimony had been completed. Chuck had brought the *Plain Dealer* with him and was reading it.

"We've had some developments," Ben said. "The defendants are talking settlement. Let's go out into the hall and find a quiet place to talk."

We found a vacant courtroom down the hall and slipped in. Ben and the clients sat at trial table, while I stood. He told them about the defendants' offer. By meeting our demand, they were finally capitulating—at least, that's what I thought.

"Why are they doing this now?" Marie asked. Her eyes were serious, and she seemed genuinely perplexed by the new offer.

"I would say that they're worried about a big award against them. The other thing is that Travelers Insurance—that's Burger King's insurance company—is offering money for the first time, so Liberty Mutual—that's Stillwater's insurance company—doesn't have to go it alone anymore."

"How much is Travelers paying?" Marie asked.

"I don't know the breakdown. I can find that out."

"That's okay. You can do that later. Right now, I've got to decide whether to take the offer," Marie said softly, more to herself than to the rest of us. "Am I supposed to make up my mind in the next ten minutes before the trial starts again?" I sensed irritation.

"Take all the time that you need. The judge will obviously delay the start of the trial until we've had a chance to talk this through."

"I don't know," Marie said. "I know we came up with that figure before trial when we had concerns that a jury could rule against us and we'd get nothing, but I don't feel like that's going to happen. Do you, Ben?"

"I think we'll get a verdict in our favor, but I can't rule out a defense verdict either. If we could talk to the jurors right now and know what they were thinking, this would be a whole lot easier. I can't read them any better than you can. If you want to know whether you're likely to win the case, I'd put that at 80 to 85 percent. That said, I can't predict what kind of dollar figure the jury will put on the case."

"It's not the money," Marie said. "I'd accept their offer right now if I thought the defendants had received the message, but I don't think they get it. I really don't. I'm also very upset by that Stillwater boy's testimony."

"It's your case, Marie," Ben said. "We'll drive the bus until you tell us you want to get off."

"You know what bothers me? The owner of the restaurant, Harold Stillwater, has never attended one deposition or one hearing. He probably knows next to nothing about this case. It may take a large jury verdict for him to get jolted and make his restaurants safer. If I settle, this whole thing will be swept under the carpet. That's what I'm concerned about."

As attorneys guiding our clients through litigation, we often had to be cautious, especially when liability was disputed and a jury could rule against us. When an offer reached a substantial figure, we couldn't let our egos get in the way and suggest a course that could lead to disaster. Although it had never happened to us, we'd all heard horror stories about plaintiffs who had turned down significant offers, only to have the jury rule for the defendant and award them nothing.

"Those are all good points, Marie. Putting all that aside, I would still recommend that you take the offer. There's always uncertainty and unpredictability when a jury decides the case," Ben said. "That's my professional advice, but I understand if you want to proceed to a verdict. I'll do whatever you want."

"Well, tell them that I don't want to accept the offer. I might change my mind as the afternoon wears on, but not right now."

"I'll let the judge and the defense attorneys know," Ben said.

A few minutes later, we were back in the courtroom with Rick Newman on the witness stand. Newman looked out over the courtroom with a military bearing that flowed from his dark-blue suit, spit-polished black shoes, and upright posture. After Ben asked him about his background in security, he told the jury about the information that he'd reviewed about the Burger King restaurant. He'd studied incident reports, police statistics, photographs, and all the depositions associated with our case. He'd also visited the site twice, once several months ago and then again that morning.

Ben quickly directed him to the crux of his testimony, his opinions about the security measures at this Burger King. Newman criticized the restaurant for its extremely limited security guard coverage. In his opinion, a guard should have been present any time the restaurant was open during darkness, including early morning hours as well as the evening. Video surveillance would also have been a deterrent, and it could have been monitored by the security guard, when one was present, or by a manager when the guard was not there. He also believed that a tall fence would have discouraged criminals from choosing this property, particularly because the fence limited their escape routes after the crime.

"The other thing is that all the employees need to be sensitive to security issues and the possibility of criminal acts. In a neighborhood like this, management needed to give employees some training about suspicious behavior and responses. It's not difficult, and studies show that it is effective in reducing crime on business premises."

"Did your study include any failings on the part of Burger King Corporation itself?"

"Yes. You have this large multinational corporation responsible for thousands of restaurants across the United States and the world. They have an operation manual. They have a section labeled 'security' in their three-ring notebook, and it's blank. There's nothing in it. This corporation has the resources to provide all types of guidance to its operators about protecting customers, but they chose not to—for some inexplicable reason. The manual provides suggestions on how to reduce the loss of inventory, discourage employee theft, and protect the physical building, but it completely ignores customer security measures."

"Did this fall below normal standards for a company like this?"

"Absolutely. This was negligent."

"Nothing further."

John Rasmussen approached the podium with a yellow pad and a thick folder in hand. He smiled and introduced himself to the expert, telling him that he represented the franchisee in this case. He began his cross-examination by gaining small admissions from the witness: confirming that Newman had never been employed by a restaurant chain to provide security services, that his former security work experience was limited to a department store and a hotel, and that his current company was a consulting firm.

"Just so the jury is clear, you aren't some neutral individual chosen by all the parties, both plaintiff and defendants, to evaluate the security at this Burger King. Correct?"

"No, I was not chosen by agreement of all attorneys."

"The judge didn't ask you to provide opinions for the jury?"

"That is correct."

"You were hired by the plaintiffs to render opinions in this case?"

"They hired me to investigate the matter and provide them with conclusions, so yes."

"Mr. Miraldi and Mr. Barrett are paying you for your services?"

"They are paying me for my time and my expenses."

"This is not the first court case that you have been involved in, is it?"

"No, I get calls from all over the country to analyze security issues."

"You mean that plaintiff attorneys across the country ask you whether a business failed to provide adequate security after a criminal has attacked a customer?"

"Yes, I do get involved in those cases and many others—employee stealing, inventory control, those sorts of things."

"Sounds like you are a jack-of-all-trades," Rasmussen said, smiling and glancing at the jury.

"Well, as long as you mean security issues, yes."

"By the way, what do you charge for your consulting services?"

"Three hundred fifty dollars an hour plus expenses."

"Do you know how much you have billed in this case?"

"No, I haven't added it up yet," Newman said, unruffled by this series of questions.

I'd also used this tactic to cross-examine expert witnesses, and it was a good way to remind the jury to approach the expert's opinions with some degree of skepticism. The law allowed parties to call an expert if the expert had specialized knowledge that could help the jurors understand something outside their own experience. Some cases became a battle between expert witnesses, and the expert with the most impressive credentials often prevailed. In our case, neither defendant had hired a security consultant to counter Newman's opinions. Thus, it was imperative for the defense to discredit him in some way.

Rasmussen began chipping away. He forced Newman to admit that crimes still occurred when a security guard was present, when video surveillance cameras were in use, when employees had received security training, and when a property was surrounded by a fence.

"In your review of this case, did you learn that two men had approached Mrs. Grossman at the drive-thru at my client's restaurant?"

"Yes, I saw the police reports and read Mrs. Grossman's deposition."

"Were you aware that the police claimed that these same two men may have been responsible for a dozen other abductions at restaurant drive-thrus in this area?"

"I know that they were convicted of at least three," Newman replied.

"There were others that the police never tied to them, were there not?"

"I don't know, but I'll take your word for it," Newman said.

"These types of crimes at a drive-thru are not unheard-of in the restaurant industry, are they?"

"No, unfortunately they're not."

"This Burger King is not the only fast-food restaurant where this type of criminal behavior has occurred?"

"Correct."

"It happens all over the country?"

"It does occur elsewhere, yes."

"Are all of these other restaurants negligent for allowing this to occur?"

"I don't know. I'd have to examine each one to answer that."

It was a strong point, and I studied the jurors to see their reactions. No one nodded, but Rasmussen had their attention.

"You testified that you inspected my client's property twice, is that correct?"

"Yes."

"Did you ever go at night?"

"No."

"A well-illuminated parking lot discourages crime, doesn't it?"

"Yes, it does."

"So you couldn't say how illuminated the back parking lot was?"

"I counted the number of light poles and light fixtures, so I have a pretty good idea," Newman answered evenly.

"Well, was it well illuminated?"

"I thought it could have had a few more lights, but I didn't put that in my report. I thought they were adequate, but there could have been more," Newman said. I was beginning to feel anxious, concerned that our witness was venturing beyond his reported findings.

"Even though it was dark, the light was bright enough for Mrs. Grossman to positively identify the man who shot her, right?" Rasmussen asked.

"Yes, that's correct," Newman said. After a pause, he added, "But as I recall his face was just inches away from hers and the menu board was illuminated." My nervousness abated for the moment.

"Did you study other fast-food restaurants in the area to see what security measures they employed?" Rasmussen asked, changing topics.

"No, that was not necessary."

"So it wasn't necessary to see what a restaurant up the street was doing?"

"I know what is demanded by the circumstances. I'd make the same recommendations for a restaurant in Detroit or Newark if it was located in a high-crime neighborhood."

"Let's say a nearby fast-food restaurant had a fence around its parking lot. Wouldn't it be important to know if crime was actually reduced there?"

"I suppose so."

"It would tell you if a fence actually discouraged crime in this setting, wouldn't it?"

"It could," Newman said, trying not to be cornered.

"In your two trips to the Hough neighborhood, did you happen to drive by a McDonald's restaurant a few blocks away—that does have a fence surrounding its parking lot?"

"No, I don't remember that," Newman said. My heart quickened as I suspected Rasmussen was ready to spring a trap.

"Mr. Newman, I have photographs of the restaurant and crime statistics for it—"

"Objection, no foundation," Ben said.

"Sustained," Judge Lawther ruled. Rasmussen could not question the witness about photographs or crime statistics that had not yet been identified or authenticated by a witness.

"I'll move on to another topic, Your Honor," Rasmussen said calmly. He'd delivered his message. The jury could connect the dots and conclude that the fence had not reduced crime at this nearby restaurant.

"Do you know if the other nearby fast-food restaurants employed security guards?"

"No, I don't."

"And if they did, you wouldn't know what hours the security guards worked?"

"No."

"You don't know if nearby restaurants had video surveillance cameras?"

"No."

"If they did, one would expect a reduction in crime at these locations?"

"Yes."

"But you didn't look at specific nearby restaurants to see what security measures they used or if they were more successful in preventing crime at their locations?"

"No, I didn't do that."

"While we're on the subject of video cameras, it's not enough to have the cameras; you need an employee—someone located inside—constantly looking at the monitor screen for the system to detect a crime. Isn't that true?"

"Well, yes and no. We've even set up dummy cameras just to discourage would-be criminals from coming onto a property. The bad guys will go someplace else if they see a camera."

"But can we agree that you have no hard data pulled from nearby restaurants that support your opinions?"

"That's not how it's done. My opinions are based on industry standards, nationwide standards if you will, that have proven effective."

"Please just answer my question. You have no concrete evidence pulled from neighborhood businesses that prove that your recommendations would have prevented this crime, do you?"

"No, not from neighborhood business crime statistics."

After this response, Rasmussen sat down, and I was relieved that he was finally finished. I thought he'd made significant headway against our expert. If the jury wanted to ignore Newman's opinions, he'd given them a basis. I also thought that Rasmussen had created some momentum for his side and that Liberty Mutual might scale down its settlement offer.

While these thoughts passed through my mind, Frank Soldat was attempting to discredit Newman's opinion that his client should have provided security guidelines in its operations manual. Claiming that each location required its own unique security plan, Soldat pressed Newman to concede that a uniform approach would be both ineffective and impractical. Newman held firm, pointing out that other companies provided standard guidelines despite the differences inherent in various locations. Newman continued to harp on the Burger King manual with the empty pages behind the security tab. It certainly appeared that the company had intended to address security but hadn't yet done so.

On redirect, Ben asked our expert a few questions to bolster his opinions against the franchisee. Ben's questions gave Newman an opportunity to explain why nationwide standards were a sound basis for his findings about this restaurant. Crime was crime, and criminal behavior did not change between areas of the country. If security measures worked in one large city, they worked in another.

The judge had delayed the afternoon recess to allow the attorneys to complete their examination of Rick Newman, and it was 3:15 by the time we finally took our break. We intended to call Chuck as our last witness that day. As we stood, Marie said to Ben, "I've reached a resolution."

"What's that?" he asked.

"I'll take their settlement offer on one condition," she said. "And this condition is very important to me."

I guessed that she wanted the restaurant to make certain changes to its security measures, a condition that would be expensive, unwieldy, and rejected. But that was not what she sought.

"I want a meeting with Harold Stillwater," she said firmly.

A few minutes later, the case was settled. Burger King added a condition of its own—the settlement figure would remain confidential, never to be made public. But Marie would get her meeting.

21

DELIVERING A MESSAGE

It had seemed like such a simple request when she'd made it, but now John Rasmussen was apprehensive. When Marie Grossman had demanded a meeting with Harold Stillwater to conclude the settlement, Rasmussen had assumed that she would be accompanied by at least one of her attorneys. However, that was not happening. He'd received a call from David Miraldi yesterday saying that he was unavailable and Marie didn't want to cancel.

"I'm sorry to call you at the last minute, but I have to cover a pretrial for another attorney," Miraldi had said. "I talked to Marie about postponing the meeting, but she feels quite capable of handling it herself. She hadn't expected me to say anything anyway, so she'll be coming alone."

Rasmussen hadn't protested. It hadn't seemed like a big deal at the time, but now—thirty minutes before the 2:30 meeting—he could sense a disaster looming. Harold Stillwater was a strong-willed businessman, and Marie Grossman was probably going to give him a piece of her mind. Although he could intervene if his own client got hot, he didn't think this would be possible with Marie. She wasn't his client, and he'd be powerless to take any action.

He'd asked Stillwater to show up fifteen minutes early to talk and go over the nature of the meeting, but he'd just received a message that his client was running late. To compound matters, Mrs. Grossman was already in his waiting room. His secretary had offered her a beverage, but she'd declined. If Stillwater was late, Rasmussen would probably just skip the conference with him and get this over with.

When Stillwater arrived a little after 2:30, Rasmussen was already in the waiting room, explaining to Marie that they would be starting a little bit late. As the large man walked into the waiting room and pulled off his raincoat, he seemed to bring the cold autumn air with him.

"Sorry I'm late," he said to Rasmussen.

Not certain that his client had noticed Marie sitting in a chair, he said, "Mr. Stillwater, this is Marie Grossman."

Stillwater folded his raincoat over his left arm and extended his right hand. "Hello, Mrs. Grossman. I'm sorry to be late; I got into a phone conversation that lasted longer than I ever thought it would."

Marie said nothing but rose stiffly from her chair.

Nothing to do but start the meeting, Rasmussen thought. "Well, let's go into my office and talk," he said. He led the way while Marie and Stillwater followed.

After Rasmussen directed Marie and Stillwater to sit in the only two chairs in his office, he sat behind his desk. It was only then that Rasmussen noticed that Marie held a large expandable folder on her lap. She looked about the room as if searching for something she'd misplaced. Stillwater sat with his hands folded on his lap, not appearing concerned in the least.

Rasmussen rubbed his hands together and placed them on his desk. "Well, Mrs. Grossman, you have requested this meeting with Mr. Stillwater." Looking at his client, he continued, "We have agreed to listen to Mrs. Grossman this afternoon and hear what she has to say." He took a deep breath and expelled the air. "We are not here to dispute with Mrs. Grossman."

Stillwater nodded his understanding, and Rasmussen hoped his client understood the import of his last statement. Again, he felt anxious and wished that one of Mrs. Grossman's attorneys were here to help referee this contest. Mrs. Grossman pulled a yellow pad from her file. If this was going to degenerate into a shouting match, he'd find out soon.

Marie sat upright in her chair. She began, "Thank you, Mr. Stillwater, for meeting with me this afternoon. I'm sure you weren't very happy that I sued you and your companies. It was good of you to come."

Stillwater raised his eyebrows, nodded, but said nothing.

Marie continued, "When we reached the settlement several weeks ago, I'd never met you. My attorneys had never met you. I felt the need to talk with you directly to discuss my concerns about your restaurant and to make sure you knew exactly what happened to me. My hope is that you will make improvements on your properties so this won't happen to someone else in the future."

Marie paused for a moment. "One thing that upset me at trial was that your son claimed that he'd gone to the building department to get a permit for a fence to increase the security at the restaurant. He said that the building department people delayed his application with red tape. We brought in the building department employee with the complete file on your property. There was no record of any request for a fence, no application, and no telephone summaries. Nothing. I would like you to talk to your son about this. I won't say more."

Rasmussen's memory returned to the courtroom. When Ron Stillwater had testified about seeking approval for a fence, he'd been surprised by the testimony. The younger Stillwater had never told him about this, and he couldn't understand why he hadn't disclosed it earlier. The next morning, when Ben Barrett had called the building department employee, he'd tried to maintain a poker face during the testimony. However, it became harder and harder for him to show no emotion as Barrett methodically asked the man to describe every paper in the file—formal papers, memos, and summaries of telephone conversations—none of which had anything to do with a fence.

He had wondered how he was going to defend the case now. He was sure that the jury believed that Ron Stillwater had invented the story. Whether he had or not, it sure looked that way. Their credibility had been destroyed, and the same message had kept repeating in his head: *It's over. It's over.* Fortunately, the Liberty Mutual adjuster, Andy Wargo, had been in the courtroom and had witnessed the same turn of events. They'd talked during the first break. Both were convinced that their defense had become a train wreck.

Soldat had scrounged up a little money from Travelers, while Andy had phoned the home office and eventually received authority to meet the rest of the plaintiff's demand. He'd been shocked when Mrs. Grossman had initially turned down the offer. When she'd agreed on the condition that they could arrange this meeting, they'd averted one disaster, but now another one was brewing.

"Okay, I'll do that," the elder Stillwater said.

"Thank you," Marie replied. She then brought out a legal pad from her folder. Glancing at the front page, she continued, "If we hadn't settled the case, I had planned to ask my attorneys to allow me to make my own closing argument."

Rasmussen's face betrayed his surprise. He'd heard of criminal defendants taking over their own defense, but never a plaintiff in a civil case.

As if reading his expression, Marie said, "I'm an attorney, so I doubt I would have said anything objectionable."

He nodded.

Marie continued, "If I had been given the opportunity, this is what I would have said." She then looked down at her notes and began her "closing argument." For the next twenty minutes, she summarized how the two men had terrorized her at Stillwater's restaurant, the medical treatment that followed, and how the injuries had affected both her and her family. As she talked, Rasmussen conceded that she was delivering a powerful statement, one that would probably have moved the jurors. Stillwater remained quiet and stoic throughout the presentation.

When she finished, Stillwater had tears in his eyes. He stood up and asked Marie, "Can I give you a hug?"

Marie rose from her chair, and the large man enveloped her in his arms. Rasmussen watched as the man known for his spontaneous acts of generosity told Marie that he was sorry for what had happened to her and told her that his company was already making changes. For her part, Marie acknowledged that no one at his restaurant had intended for any of this to occur.

"I really appreciate your conciliatory words," she replied.

After they'd both left, Rasmussen felt an enormous sense of relief. In addition, he was also trying to process what he had just seen. Would Marie have ever filed this lawsuit if Stillwater had visited her soon after the shooting? He doubted it.

✧ ✧ ✧

Rasmussen never expected to see Marie again, but then, about a year later, she was walking down Detroit Road as he was about to enter the White Door Saloon for lunch. The White Door was just two blocks from his Lakewood office building and a favorite place for the office people to grab a quick soup or sandwich. Marie and he greeted each other, and each asked how the other was doing.

"You know, I'm glad we eventually got your case resolved," he said.

Marie smiled. "Do you know what I've been doing with the settlement money?"

"I've never really thought that was any of my business."

"Well, I call it my 'Feel-Good Fund.' Whenever I see a newspaper account about someone who's down on their luck and needs financial help, I write a check from the settlement money."

"Over the years, I'll probably pay out millions of dollars in insurance settlements, and I kind of doubt anybody else will ever do that," he said.

"Maybe they will, but you'll just never know about it."

Part III

Redemption

22

THE ANGER

1996

The late January air stung their faces as Marie and Chuck opened the car doors. The shopping center's parking lot had been cleared of snow a few days earlier, but patches of ice still booby-trapped the black asphalt surface. Marie held Chuck's elbow as they moved with heads down toward the movie theater. Once they were inside, the cinema lobby smelled of wool, popcorn, and perfume. On this Friday evening, the theater had attracted mainly young people, in either quiet pairs or noisy packs. Marie doubted that many of them were buying tickets for *Dead Man Walking*, the movie she and Chuck had come to view.

After purchasing their tickets, they walked into a small side theater and joined a dozen other patrons who were scattered about the hundred or so seats. While a preview was playing, they chose seats next to the aisle in the back half of the room. Once the film began, the two found themselves captivated from the first scene. As the movie neared its conclusion, Chuck glanced over at Marie, who was crying.

"Do you want to leave?" he asked.

"No, I'm all right. It's just very moving."

"Something's bothering you. What is it?"

"I'll tell you after the movie."

When the movie finished, Chuck heard Marie let out a long breath. He could see that she had stopped crying, but her face looked drained.

He decided to wait until they got into the car to find out what had triggered such a reaction.

"Was the movie a little too close to home?" he asked as he pulled the car onto the city street. A gust of wind shook the car, and he gripped the steering wheel to keep it in its lane.

"One part was," she answered, looking out the passenger window.

Chuck expected to hear more, but Marie did not continue, and they drove in silence for a few more minutes.

"What part moved you so much?" he asked.

"It was when the murdered boy's father was talking to the nun about the killer."

Chuck thought back to that scene. The boy's family had felt betrayed when the nun fought to get the killer's death sentence commuted to life imprisonment.

"What about that?" he asked.

Marie hesitated for a moment before answering. "Do you remember what the father said to the nun? He said, 'I am filled with so much hate.' And I just started to cry."

"I don't quite understand," Chuck said.

"I suddenly realized how angry I still am. Even today I'm filled with hate for that man. It's been eight years, and I can't let go of my anger. That father expressed the emotion that I feel."

"I don't know if there is anything wrong with that feeling," Chuck said, taking his eyes off of the road to glance at Marie.

Marie was looking straight ahead. "That movie was like a mirror, and I didn't like what I saw," she said, her words just above a whisper.

✵ ✵ ✵

Marie didn't know why she occasionally listened to talk radio while she was driving. She almost never agreed with the radio host or any of the misguided callers. Maybe she just wanted to know what other people were thinking, or perhaps she was intrigued by the callers' shocking comments. Today, people were talking about what attracted them to perennial presidential hopeful Pat Buchanan.

As one caller droned on about the problems in America's cities, he said, "I agree with Pat. If you want to solve these problems, you just need to lock and load. That's the answer, plain and simple."

The caller's voice was loud, forceful, and angry. *He thinks he's coming off tough and strong, but he sounds weak, even pathetic,* Marie thought. Then her brain made the connection. Did she sound like this when she talked about Thompson? When she thought about him?

How many times had she fantasized about Thompson approaching her house, walking up the back steps, and attempting to break in? She always imagined that she had a handgun within reach and she used it. Thompson's face would be superimposed on a target and she would shoot him—bull's-eye. Sometimes it was not him that she fantasized about hurting. It could be any criminal about to attack her. Not that she would ever stalk anyone or seek out a confrontation, but if the opportunity arose, she would shoot and kill in self-defense.

These fantasies fueled a feeling of power. The world's bad guys would never mess with her again, not ever. However, the radio caller's boastful rant had repulsed her. She had seen through him immediately. Stripped of his false bravado, the man was weak. For the second time in several weeks, she had glimpsed herself through someone else. Didn't she dream of a chance to "lock and load"? Was that the person she'd become? She didn't know. But she would work this out—later.

✿ ✿ ✿

"I don't know if I'm up to that," Marie answered.

"You'd be perfect," her friend Susan Umbernour replied. "People need to hear from a victim who's fought back. Your message would end the evening on a positive note."

"Susan, I'm not a victim, and I refuse to be labeled as one. If you want me to speak for victims, I don't represent them. I'm a person who was shot. That's all."

"Oh, Marie, that was a poor choice of words. I know you're not a victim. You refused to let the men get into your car. That took courage. Let me start over. We want someone with your perspective and insight to talk about your experience."

"Let me think about it. I am very reluctant to do this," Marie replied.

"Please consider it. It's important that people think about this. The world likes to pretend that there's no violence directed toward women. If we talk about it, publicize it, then we are working to make the world a better place."

"You're making it hard for me to say no," Marie said.

"So is that a yes? Sister Anita will be very pleased."

"I'll let you know in a few days."

In 1980, an Ursuline nun from Cleveland had been raped and murdered by El Salvador national guardsmen while serving as a missionary in that war-torn country. The crime had shocked the Cleveland community and the country at large. Since then members of her order periodically organized events to honor their slain sister. This year they were organizing an event at Public Square called the Women's Watch Vigil. Not only would this event honor their sister, but it would also force the community to remember that violence against women was all too prevalent and exempted no one. After further reflection, Marie agreed to speak. When she called Susan with her decision, she reiterated that she would only participate if the organizers never referred to her as a victim.

For the next three weeks, Marie struggled with her message. The first part was easy. She would talk about what had happened to her. She had been shot in the head at point-blank range. The bullet had missed her brain but destroyed her jaw. She would tell the crowd that she could now talk and live an almost normal life because of superb medical care. Her assailants had been identified, captured, and convicted—and were in prison, where they could not harm her or others. Her family and friends had loved and cared for her, giving her the strength to face and recover from four jaw surgeries and months of painful rehabilitation. She would tell everyone that she viewed herself as very fortunate.

But there was also her anger. Did she want to admit this to a large crowd of strangers? If she did, what would it reveal about her? Would her anger do anything to advance anyone's understanding? She didn't know.

When the day of the event came, Marie was apprehensive. She had prepared her remarks. They were typed out on three pages.

Public Square, the center of downtown Cleveland, was four large city blocks that had originally been set aside for farm animals when the city was first laid out in 1796 by settlers from Connecticut. Today, Terminal Tower, a fifty-two-story office building constructed in 1927, was the major player in the square, competing with a large hotel, a Civil War monument, and several other office buildings for domination. The spring evening was cool and crisp. Because of this, Marie had dressed warmly, not wanting the chill to put a tremor in her voice. Several hundred people had gathered around a podium and sound system set up for the event.

When it was Marie's turn to speak, she walked briskly to the microphone and held her papers in her hands. She told the crowd how lucky she was to have survived the shooting and recovered as well as she had. She then turned to the difficult part of her speech.

"The physical healing took about two years, but I haven't healed emotionally and spiritually. There's a place inside that's still raw. And that's what I really want to talk to you about tonight."

For the next few minutes, Marie told her listeners that she had fantasized about shooting her assailant in the jaw. "In part, this is pure revenge," she explained, "but there is something else going on as well. I've wanted to feel strong, to be strong. To think and act strong is how I am preserving my sense of self.

"There's another side to this 'You can't hurt me' attitude, and two recent events have helped me see this more clearly." She told her audience about her reaction to the movie *Dead Man Walking* and to the radio caller who had boasted about his "lock and load" solution to America's problems. "These responses are not strong at all. They are weak, even pathetic," she explained.

Marie turned to the dilemma that she was trying to resolve. For weeks she had been struggling with her anger. It was not the way she wanted to be, yet it was the only thing that made her feel that she was in control. She would lose something if she just gave up her anger and accepted what had happened to her. She would lose her self-respect, and she would never do that. "I want to be better than this. I don't want to go around with a concealed weapon, always on guard and ready to defend myself. I can be better.

"On the other hand, we live in a time when you can be shot at Burger King or when a nun can be murdered within yards of where she lives. So how do we, as women, take care of ourselves without sinking to the level of those who would harm us, without being consumed with anger and fear?"

Marie looked up from her speech and surveyed the crowd. She sensed that they were acutely tuned into her message and ready to receive an answer to the weighty question that she had just raised. She faltered for a moment, knowing that her answer would disappoint.

"I wanted so much to end my remarks tonight with some words of wisdom, with an answer that would help us move to another level. Believe me, I've struggled to do that. But I'm just not there yet. Perhaps by coming together and telling our stories, we'll figure it out. I'm grateful for the opportunity to participate here tonight. Thank you."

She folded her papers and walked away to quiet applause.

23

AN UNEXPECTED TURN

1997

The question Marie had posed a year ago in her Public Square speech had faded. Although she had intended to search out books and articles about anger, she had not. Instead, her life had been filled with activity as she juggled family, friends, and her consulting business. She occasionally thought about Richard Thompson and whether he would be granted parole at his next hearing. That possibility no longer overwhelmed her, nor did she dwell on it. Yes, she would feel anxious, but she would soon be absorbed by other things and the unease would pass. Her life had returned to a fulfilling rhythm.

When she awoke one March morning, she was astonished by a thought that had surfaced. The idea had seemingly come from nowhere, but there it was, front and center, unwilling to be dismissed. As she grasped that this was her journey's final step, she felt calm and at peace. For reasons not altogether clear, she needed to go to the prison and talk to Thompson. This was not just an option; it was an imperative.

A few minutes later, she walked into the kitchen, where Chuck was eating a bowl of cereal and reading the morning newspaper. When she told him what she wanted to do, he folded the newspaper and dropped it onto the floor.

"I don't think that's a good idea," he told her, trying to remain calm. "Going to the prison, unloading your anger on this guy, is dangerous."

"That's not it at all. It's hard to explain, but I feel like this meeting will complete the healing process. I want to speak to him as a person. I need to see for myself who he is, why he shot me, whether he still thinks about that night, and whether he's changed. The two of us are always going to be connected because of what happened at Burger King, and we should talk about it."

Chuck thought the whole idea sounded crazy. Richard Thompson had shot his wife in the head and had spent the last nine years in prison because of that. He was a hardened criminal who, in his warped logic, probably blamed Marie for what had happened to him. What was Marie thinking—that they could go into a prison meeting room and have a normal conversation?

"What makes you think Thompson will want to talk to you?" Chuck asked. "You're probably the last person he'd want to see in prison, or anywhere for that matter."

"I have to find out."

"Marie, this guy held a loaded thirty-eight-caliber handgun to your head and fired it. He was an angry young man back then, and he's probably angrier now after years in prison."

Marie sat down at the kitchen table and looked into her husband's eyes. "I'm not going to do this recklessly. Before I ever step inside that prison, I'll find out what kind of person he is now—you know, make sure he's not some ranting, crazy man. If I decide that this visit will make him more likely to harm me once he's out, I won't go. Remember, he pled guilty to the charges, testified against his friend, and apologized to me in open court. I have a feeling—a gut feeling—that he will want to talk to me. I don't know why, but I think he'll want to explain why the gun went off. And if he doesn't want to talk to me, well then, that will be it."

After more than thirty years of marriage, Chuck knew that once Marie set her mind to do something—whether it was to climb Mount Kilimanjaro or revamp the Cleveland school system—you had to let her try. He was sure that Thompson would refuse to meet with her and this scheme would fall apart on its own.

"I have strong reservations, but if you think you need to do this, then do it," Chuck replied.

That morning Marie began by calling the parole office, whose employees regularly sent her notices about Thompson's upcoming hearings and the board's decisions. After being switched from one person to the next, she finally talked to someone who told her to call the Office of Victim Services, an agency under the umbrella of the Ohio Department of Rehabilitation and Correction.

When she got through to that office, Marie asked if the Office of Victim Services could arrange meetings between prisoners and the persons they had harmed. She still refused to call herself a victim.

"Yes, we will eventually be able to do that," the administrative assistant told her. "However, the program is not yet operational. We're working on procedures and guidelines right now. We should have it up and running by early next year, sometime in 1998. You can call back in a few months and check our progress."

"Next year won't work for me," Marie replied. "Richard Thompson, the man who shot me, has a parole hearing next month, and if he's granted parole, he could be released soon after that. I need to talk to him while he's still in prison."

"Why is it so important that you meet with Mr. Thompson right before his parole hearing?" the assistant asked. Marie could sense that the woman was suspicious of her motives.

"For the last nine years, I've been trying to heal from this event both physically and emotionally," Marie said evenly. "I don't know if you can understand this, but I need this meeting for closure. Believe me, I'm approaching this meeting in a spirit of reconciliation."

"I still think you should call back in a few months. We're just not ready to facilitate meetings yet. There's a good chance Mr. Thompson will still be incarcerated then."

"Who is in charge of the program?" Marie asked.

"Her name is Karin Ho," the employee answered.

"I would like Ms. Ho to give me a call."

"I'm not trying to be difficult," the administrative assistant said. "We need to implement screening procedures for both victims and inmates. Then we need to develop guidelines for the actual meetings. We just had the money appropriated for this a few months ago. I hope you can understand that these things take time. We've got to be very organized before any victim meets an inmate. If we don't, somebody could get hurt and this program would be scrapped."

"I'm not trying to be difficult either. I'm hoping you can make an exception for me before all of the procedures are in place. I'm an attorney, and I doubt you'd need to do much screening for me."

"I'll leave your name and phone number for Ms. Ho," the employee said.

"When do you think she'll get back to me?" Marie asked.

"She's not in today, but I think you should hear from her in a few days."

"I'd appreciate that," Marie said, trying to hide her disappointment and irritation.

"And although I know you wouldn't try, you can't visit an inmate on your own. You have to go through this program. It's the only way."

"Uh-huh," Marie replied. She thought about telling the assistant that she had no intention of doing that, but the assistant's warning irked her and she decided not to respond.

After a few moments of silence, the assistant spoke again. "Mrs. Grossman, please don't feel impatient. Karin will call you. She's a victim herself and has walked in your shoes. If she can, she'll help you. She's a very caring person."

"Thank you," Marie said as she hung up the phone.

She poured herself a cup of tea, walked into the living room, and sat down in a cushioned chair. The last phone call had sapped her energy. She realized that she would have to cut through bureaucratic red tape to make this meeting happen. However, she would remain hopeful and wait for the return phone call.

After four days had passed without her hearing from Karin Ho, Marie decided to call back. In a polite but firm manner, she would reinforce that this meeting was critically important to her. The same assistant answered the phone and explained that Karin Ho was not in the office. She assured Marie that her boss had not forgotten her and was planning to talk to the warden first and then the prisoner. Although they could make no guarantees, they were trying to make an exception for her. "Believe me, we are working on it. We'll be in touch," the assistant told her.

Over the next few weeks, Marie considered other ways to force the meeting if the Office of Victim Services did not arrange it. She made a list of influential people who might intervene for her if she contacted them. She even considered arranging a press conference to draw attention to her plight but realized that this was too drastic. She would be patient for another several weeks before making her next move.

* * *

A few weeks after initiating her request for a prison visit, Marie attended a local seminar that addressed violence in America. One female speaker in particular seemed to talk to her directly, and when the presenter asked for questions, Marie's hand shot up. After the speaker recognized her, Marie stood to ask her question.

"If the prison officials let you speak to Joseph Vacarro, what would you say to him?" Marie asked.

The speaker was Debbie Morris, a woman who had been raped, brutalized, and left for dead by Robert Willie and his accomplice Joseph Vacarro. Willie's story had become the basis for the book and movie *Dead Man Walking*. Morris's gripping testimony had been instrumental in sending Willie to death row and Vacarro to a life in prison without parole. Morris told the jury that Willie had proposed stuffing her into the trunk of a car and burning her alive, but she had survived to tell her story.

"I don't know. I haven't got to that yet. I'll figure that out after he agrees to talk to me. I just know I have to do it," Morris responded.

Marie felt validated. Here was a woman who had been brutalized and now felt the overwhelming need to talk to the man who had harmed her. Like Marie, she was unsure of what she would say to him. She just wanted the opportunity to have that dialogue.

Several days later, the assistant from the Office of Victim Services called. Richard Thompson's parole had been granted, and he would be released on or after June 9, 1997. Their office was still trying to arrange a meeting with Thompson before his release.

"Today is April eighteenth," Marie said. "Time's running out."

"You'll hear from us in a week," the assistant assured her.

A week went by, and Marie did not receive a call from either Ho or her assistant. Marie phoned and left a message, but no one returned her call.

In May, Marie began looking into ways that she could speed up the process and put pressure on government officials to allow the meeting. In the middle of the month, she sent three letters to state officials, two at the Ohio Department of Rehabilitation and Correction and one at the Department of Public Safety. She explained who she was, what had happened to her, and that she wanted closure before her assailant was released from prison in a few weeks. None of the state officials responded to her letters.

✵ ✵ ✵

Frank Malone sat across from Richard Thompson in one of the prison's small conference rooms. Malone was in his early forties with short-cropped black curly hair and a receding hairline. A former probation officer, Malone had been one of the prison's case managers for the past twelve years. He had been Thompson's CM ever since Thompson had arrived at Southeastern Correctional Institution in 1988. Malone was street smart; he'd grown up in one of Columbus's tough neighborhoods and, like Thompson, had been a standout athlete. Malone had been a bruising running back at East High School and, unlike Thompson, stayed out of trouble. He'd received a full ride to play football at Bowling Green State University, where he'd earned a degree in criminal justice. A weight lifter, he still looked like he could break tackles and knock over any defensive back who got in his way.

Malone studied the tall prisoner, who walked with a swagger when around other inmates but who now allowed his shoulders to slump as he waited for Malone to address him. Thompson no longer looked like an athlete. Unlike many of the younger prisoners, Thompson did not exercise, and his lean body had grown fat on the high-calorie prison food.

"I've got something to talk to you about," Malone said. Thompson folded his hands in his lap and looked bored, but Malone sensed that Thompson was anxious to know why his CM had pulled him off his job to talk to him.

"I received a call from Victim Services, and they asked me to talk to you about what they call a prisoner-victim dialogue," Malone continued.

"A what?" Thompson said, pressing his palms together and rubbing them against each other in a circular motion.

"Here it is. The woman you shot wants to talk to you before you get released."

Thompson's bored expression instantly vanished. "She wants to mess with my parole, doesn't she? Don't bullshit me. That's what this is all about, right?"

Malone had developed a rapport with this prisoner over the past nine years, and Thompson seemed to trust him about as much as any prisoner could trust his case manager. When Thompson had first arrived at Southeastern, Malone was charged with integrating him into the prison setting, periodically assessing him, and suggesting programs that could benefit him.

"No, that's not it at all," Malone told him.

"I've played by the rules, kept myself out of trouble, and I don't want nothin' that could screw things up for me. I've come too far."

"Yes, you have come pretty far," Malone agreed. He remembered the drug-dependent prisoner who was always getting into fights with other inmates when he first arrived. The guy who didn't believe that he had to follow rules and whose behavior consistently landed him in the hole. Most of these incidents stemmed from Thompson's penny-ante business of selling cigarettes and snacks to other inmates, something prohibited by the prison rules. Thompson would "sell" a bag of chips to a prisoner today if he agreed to repay him with two bags of chips in several weeks. If the inmate didn't pay him back, Thompson beat him up. Whenever he was discovered—because of either a "sale" or an ensuing fight—he landed in solitary confinement.

"Are you telling me that I have to do this in order to get out in June?" Thompson asked.

"No, I'm not. Whether you meet with her or not will not affect your parole."

Thompson looked around the small room as if others were listening in. "Why does she want to see me right now? I been in here nine years, and this is the first time I've ever heard of this. Something ain't right."

"Do you trust me?" Malone asked.

"Should I?" Thompson shot back.

"This woman wants closure. Do you know what that means?"

"Yeah, I know what that means."

"She wants to ask you some questions. Find out why you did what you did."

"How do I know that she don't just want to jump over the table and choke me?"

Malone started laughing. To Thompson, it sounded put-on.

"What's so funny? It's my freedom we're talking about."

"I just was trying to picture this little old lady jumping over the table and taking a swing at you," Malone said, raising his eyebrows and nodding at Thompson.

The prisoner smiled but said nothing as he continued to think about the requested meeting. Finally, Thompson broke the silence. "I ain't doing this if I don't get something in writing that this won't screw up my parole."

"So you'll do it then if we get that in writing?" Malone asked.

"I didn't say that, did I?" Thompson snapped. "All I'm saying is that I might do it if I get that in writing. I still need to think about this. I can't make no snap decision."

"Look it, I told you this before. You're better than all this. Your mom and dad taught you to be better than this," Malone said, playing a card he knew would have an effect on the man.

Thompson's crime had shamed his parents, both of whom had thought their son would eventually go to college on a basketball scholarship and make them proud. His mom was a high school teacher, while his dad had been a security guard at the same school. Thompson had come from a good home where his working-poor parents had provided for his needs. Until he was fourteen, he'd gone to church every Sunday with his mom and siblings. His dad, a youth basketball coach at the YMCA, had always taken his son with him to play and learn from the older boys. His dad had died while Thompson was in prison, and he had been unable to attend the funeral.

Malone's comment struck home. The man's large right hand squeezed his chin. He shook his head and let out a deep breath. "I'm no saint, but I'm no rapist either. I just wanted her to take some money out of an ATM machine—nothing else."

"You should tell her that in person," Malone said.

As if he had not heard him, Thompson continued, "I didn't intend to shoot her neither. The car jumped forward and my hand hit the door frame and it went off. I never used a gun against anybody."

"You should talk to her then," Malone said. "I know it won't be easy, but you need to do it for her and for yourself."

"Okay. I'll think about it."

"Good, I'll get something in writing."

* * *

It was a beautiful spring day in northeastern Ohio. Richard Thompson would be released in twelve days, and Marie still had no answer about a meeting. She decided to take a thirty-mile bicycle trip, hoping it would give her time to think about her alternatives, none of which seemed promising. As she pedaled, she thought about a press conference again. She could do it in a positive way, showing no anger and not criticizing the state officials who had failed her thus far.

She pedaled her bicycle into the garage, walked up the back porch steps, and opened the back door. Once in the kitchen, she drew water from the tap into a tall glass and sat down.

A few minutes later, the phone rang. It was Karin Ho. She had arranged a meeting for Marie with Richard Thompson on June 6, 1997, at the Southeastern Correctional Institution.

24

FINAL DETAILS

As she drove to the Southeastern Correctional Institution, Karin Ho thought about the upcoming dialogue between Marie Grossman and Richard Thompson. She had sensed Marie's impatience throughout the process, but Marie simply did not understand the difficulties she'd faced or realize how careful she had to be. Two days before, she'd obtained a written statement signed by a corrections official confirming that the upcoming meeting would not affect Thompson's parole. She'd told Thompson's case manager about the paper, and he'd informed Thompson that they had the verification that he'd demanded. With that, Thompson had agreed to the dialogue and the preparation session that Karin would conduct.

When Karin met him, Thompson gave her an embarrassed smile, revealing a large gap between his two front teeth. Karin thought that, except for his great size and prison uniform, Richard Thompson was not a menacing figure. Karin handed the signed statement to Thompson, who read it carefully, mouthing some of the words as he read.

"Okay. This'll work," he said.

"Are you comfortable going forward with the dialogue?" Karin asked.

"You know, everybody's telling me I'm stupid to do this."

"I'd use a different word. I'd say you're showing some courage."

Thompson squinted at Karin and raised his eyebrows. Although he said nothing, his eyes said, "Don't try to con me."

Sensing she'd lost some credibility, Karin attempted to get back on track. "Let's talk about what's going to happen on Friday."

Thompson fidgeted in his chair but remained quiet.

"Marie will be there with a friend. The assistant warden will be there, and I'll be there. Have you chosen someone to accompany you?"

"Yeah, my CM's coming with me," he said.

"Oh, that's good," Karin said. She'd expected him to bring a fellow prisoner, but it was probably better that his case manager would be attending. Had the warden made the selection for him? She wouldn't ask.

"Where's this going to take place? I know you told me, but I forgot," he said quietly.

"In the warden's conference room, just outside his office."

Thompson nodded and remembered that was what Karin had told him before.

"I want to go over the types of questions Marie is likely to ask you."

He nodded, looked down at his feet, and then returned his gaze to Karin.

"She'll want to know if you are sorry."

"I done said that at my sentencing."

"She'll want to hear it again. And she'll want to know why you shot her."

"I kind of figured that."

"She's going to tell you how your actions harmed her. Will you be ready for that?"

"Yes."

"She may want to know about your life before you committed the crime and what your prison experience has taught you."

"Okay."

For the next forty-five minutes, Karin asked Thompson these and other questions. She listened to his answers, not to change them, but to discover how he'd respond. If he got agitated or angry with her, then he was not a good candidate for the program and she'd call things off. The large man responded quietly throughout the session. When Karin left the meeting, she felt confident about Friday's dialogue.

When she returned to her office, she called Marie and updated her about her visit with Thompson.

"Marie, what questions will you have for Richard Thompson?"

"I really haven't given that much thought. I just want to engage with him as a person, find out about his past and what prison has been like, and probably go into his plans for the future."

"Is that all?" Karin asked, wondering why this woman had been so intent on setting up this meeting if this was all she was going to ask.

"Of course, I'll ask him about the night when he shot me. Why he shot me."

"If there's one subject I'd like you to focus on, it would be this: think about all the ways his actions have harmed you."

"That's not a subject I was going to get into. I don't want to sound like this angry woman," Marie answered.

"Well, we've found that it's important for an offender to understand that—all the ramifications of his actions."

"All right, I'll be ready to discuss that with him."

"Who's going with you to the dialogue? Your husband?"

"No, when you called, he already had an out-of-state commitment that can't be changed."

"Are you coming alone?"

"No. I thought about coming by myself, but I invited my friend Peggy to accompany me."

"Are you nervous?"

"Actually, just the opposite. You know, I felt so calm and relieved when you called a few days ago and told me that the meeting was going forward. I still do. I'm sure I'll get more apprehensive as the time gets closer."

Karin closed the conversation by telling Marie that she would meet her at a Bob Evans restaurant in Lancaster on the day of the meeting. They could talk again, and afterward, she would lead the way in her car onto the prison grounds.

25

THE VISIT

It was 9:30 a.m. when Marie and her friend Peggy Kuechle pulled into the Bob Evans restaurant in Lancaster, Ohio, on June 6, 1997. After two and a half hours on the road, the women were ready for a break. Although the weather had been sunny and mild, Marie had been subdued during the drive, and instead of making conversation, the two had listened to the radio for much of the journey. Karin Ho had promised to meet Marie here and answer last-minute questions. After that, her car would lead the way and Marie would follow her into the prison complex.

A short middle-aged woman was waiting on a bench inside the door and smiled at them as they entered. The woman stood up and asked, "Marie?"

Karin was smartly dressed in a black blazer and gray pants. Her light brown hair had golden highlights and was cut short. The three women walked to a table to talk and grab a cup of coffee. Karin asked if they had any questions about the meeting, and Marie shook her head.

"I don't want you to set your expectations too high," Karin said, her glasses reflecting sunlight and obscuring her eyes. "Mr. Thompson has agreed to meet with you, but don't be surprised if he doesn't say much or says something that you find offensive."

"I just want to engage with him as a person," Marie replied.

"I know you do, but this meeting is uncharted waters for him. If he becomes uncomfortable, he could become argumentative or combative.

I just want you to be aware of that possibility." Karin looked first at Marie and then at Peggy.

The women nodded.

"A couple of years back, before the legislature appropriated funds for this program, we had an unfortunate situation. A victim arranged a meeting with her assailant on her own and met him in the visitor's meeting room. He stabbed her with a makeshift knife." She looked at both women again to make sure that her words had sunk in.

Karin continued, "That's why the only way a victim can meet with a prisoner is through our program. We have screened this prisoner and believe he is a good candidate, but we have to proceed very carefully."

"I really appreciate that you were able to arrange this before he was released," Marie said. She suspected that there was a subtext to Karin's message: a meeting like this could not be rushed, even when the victim sent letters to state officials urging speedy action.

Marie and Peggy followed Karin to the prison's outer gate. A tall wrought-iron sign arched over the road with the words "WELCOME TO SOUTHEASTERN CORRECTIONAL INSTITUTION." To give the sign an Ohio flavor, the authorities had attached a silhouette of the state map on one side and a red metal cardinal on the other. The outskirts of the prison grounds were filled with evergreens and deciduous trees, and they initially blocked any view of the prison buildings.

"I feel like we're entering a college campus," Peggy said.

"Or a cemetery," Marie added.

The peaceful setting changed abruptly when the women saw a tall chain-link fence topped with barbed wire surrounding the prison's assorted brick buildings. Karin's vehicle stopped at a checkpoint, and after a brief conversation with the guard, they were all waved through. They parked their cars in a small parking lot servicing the warden's office, where the meeting would take place. It was a little after 10 a.m., and the meeting was not scheduled to begin for another half hour.

What have I gotten myself into? Marie asked herself as she climbed out of her car. Turning to Karin, Marie inquired, "Would it be okay if I just sat outside for a few minutes before I go inside?" Karin nodded and walked into the warden's office with Peggy, leaving Marie alone. For the next fifteen minutes, Marie attempted to relax by focusing on her breathing and being aware of her surroundings. She cleared her mind while she studied the nearby azaleas and rhododendrons. Feeling more composed, she walked into the warden's stand-alone building.

The warden and the assistant warden greeted her and told her that the meeting would take place in a conference room next to his office. Although the warden would not attend, his assistant would. The assistant opened the conference room door and asked them to enter. The room was simply furnished with a long mahogany table with ten cushioned chairs. Once inside, Karin took charge and sat at the head of the table, while the assistant warden drifted to the far end. Karin told Marie to sit directly to her left and suggested that Peggy take the seat next to Marie. She explained that Thompson and his companion would sit across from Marie and Peggy.

From her leather briefcase, Marie pulled out a sheet of typewritten questions and a yellow pad. Like an attorney about to begin a deposition, she slid the briefcase onto the floor by her feet and placed a pen over the legal pad. She clasped her hands, resting them on the table's surface, and waited. The assistant warden and Karin looked at some papers that they had brought with them. For the next few minutes, no one spoke. In the silence, Marie could hear the ticking of the wall clock.

There was a knock on the partially open door before it swung completely open. Framed in the doorway was Richard Thompson, and at his side stood a muscular man in a dark-blue suit. Marie recognized Thompson immediately. The face that she had struggled to remember in the hospital had not changed. He was still that tall, towering black man, but instead of having a thin and wiry build, he was now much heavier, reminding her of a football player.

Directing his attention to Karin Ho, the muscular man introduced himself as Frank Malone, Thompson's case manager, and asked where they should sit.

"Hello, Richard," Karin said, speaking to him as if they were old friends. "I'd like you to sit on the other side of the table, right across from Marie." Addressing the case manager, she said, "Mr. Malone, thanks for all of your help. I'd like you to sit right next to Richard."

Looking down at his feet, Thompson walked toward his seat, his hands hidden in the pockets of his dark-blue prison pants. Despite the room's air-conditioning, perspiration spotted his light-blue prison shirt and his forehead glistened. He quietly pulled back his chair and sat down quickly. His hands were not handcuffed, and he rubbed his palms together in a circular motion just below the table's surface. He glanced at the people sitting around the table, moving quickly from one face to the next, before resting his gaze on the table's polished surface. From this quick scan, he registered anger on Marie's face.

All morning he'd felt anxious about this meeting. He couldn't say he was scared. He'd survived nine years in prison, revealing to himself a toughness that had surprised him. But in prison, he'd learned the rules and the consequences when he'd broken one. This meeting, this place, these people—there was so much uncertainty. It unnerved him.

"Good morning, everyone. My name is Karin Ho, and I am the facilitator for this dialogue. I've had a chance to talk to both Richard and Marie before today, and you know what this is all about. If at any time anyone wants to take a break, we'll do that. Just let me know. Marie, I know you've got some things you want to talk about, so I'll let you start."

Marie was surprised that Karin's preliminary remarks were so short, and she hesitated for a moment. She began, "Richard, can I call you by your first name?"

Thompson nodded.

Marie continued, "I did not come here in anger. I want you to know that from the start. As you might imagine, I do have a lot of questions for you. I want to know about your life before all of this. I want to talk about what happened at Burger King and what was going on in your mind that night, how you feel about it today, and a number of other things."

Thompson nodded. The woman's voice was conversational, but how long would that last? He'd say something wrong—he knew it—and it would set her off. He realized now that this meeting was a mistake. He glanced over at Frank Malone, trying to get his attention, but Malone was absently cleaning his left thumbnail with his right index finger. Thompson's heart began to beat rapidly and he clenched his teeth, waiting for the first question.

"Richard, what was your life like before the shooting?" she asked.

Thompson did not answer immediately. Malone glanced up from his fingernail cleaning and looked at him impatiently. The prisoner cleared his throat.

"I've got an older brother and two younger sisters. We moved to Cleveland from Louisiana when I was about five years old 'cause my dad was looking for work." He stopped, wondering how much he should tell this woman.

"Go on," Marie urged.

"See, this wasn't supposed to happen to me," Thompson continued, pointing out the window toward one of the large prison buildings. "My mom taught me better. She made me go to church every Sunday when I was younger. In high school, I got this scholarship to play basketball at Purdue, but then I got my girlfriend pregnant and I decided to stay home and take care of her and the baby. I started hangin' out with the wrong guys in the neighborhood. I got into drugs; I stopped going to my job. I started robbin' people to get money for dope. Pretty soon, all I wanted to do was get high."

"I wasn't the first person you robbed then?" Marie asked.

Thompson looked at the assistant warden before he answered. "No, you wasn't the first," he answered.

"How long did you know Christopher Martin?"

"Him and me. I knowed him since we was in grade school."

"Were you friends?"

"Yeah, sort of. We hung out together. We did drugs together, but, you know, he's a mean one. He's one of these guys with an attitude. You don't want to cross him."

"But you testified against him."

"Yeah, that's right, I did. We did the crime. We got caught, and we both should've took our punishment. I pled guilty and he should have too—but he didn't."

Marie was asking the questions that she'd stockpiled in her brain for years. Thompson's answers and, more importantly, his demeanor would give her the missing information that she needed to judge him. Her eyes locked on his every movement.

Thompson could feel himself being drawn into something too. The other people in the room had disappeared. It was only him and this woman he'd shot.

"Why were you at the Burger King that night?"

"We'd been there a couple of hours, waiting for someone to rob. You know, we wanted money for drugs. We'd been smoking weed all day and had run out. We was waiting for one person at the drive-thru— could be a man or a woman—and we was going to get into the car with that person and have them drive us to an ATM, where they'd take out as much money as they could. Nobody was supposed to get hurt. I didn't mean to shoot you. You hit the gas and the gun went off."

For the first time, Marie's voice toughened. "You put a loaded gun to my temple, Richard. That part was no accident."

The others in the room tensed as one. They knew that Thompson's next statement could send the dialogue into a tailspin from which it would never recover.

"I am really sorry for what I done. I'm not going to blame it on the drugs. I'm the one who done it. I know that," he said. He seemed to be finished but then added, "And after the gun went off, I should've checked on you. I shouldn't have run away like that."

"Thank you for saying that," Marie said, her tone softening again. Now it was Marie's turn to pause as she contemplated her next question. "Have you ever thought about what you did to me?" she finally asked.

Based on his preparation session with the facilitator, Thompson had known this question was coming. He did not hesitate. "Yes, I have. I've thought about you over these years, and I've always hoped that you was doing okay."

"Do you want to know about my injuries and how they affected me and my family?"

"Yes."

"The bullet went through the left side of my jaw and out the right side. It shattered the jawbones and some of the little bone pieces never mended together. When my husband first saw me in the emergency room, my jaw was hanging over my chest and my face was so swollen that he could barely recognize me." Her voice was calm and stripped of any emotion.

Thompson had not been prepared for this. He could find no words and nodded to tell her to go on.

"I had four surgeries in all. Two bone grafts from my hip to my jaw, plates screwed in, and some plastic surgeries. I was wired shut after each surgery. I vomited the first night in the hospital after the surgery. That was really scary with my jaw wired shut and no place for the vomit to go. I was always afraid that I would get sick. After the first surgery, I had a tracheostomy, a hole in my throat to help me breathe."

"I didn't know any of that," Thompson said, his voice almost a whisper.

Over the next five minutes, Marie told him about the limitations that she would always have. Nerve damage had eliminated her sense of taste and her ability to lift her tongue. Despite the bone grafts and plates in her jaw, it did not open a normal distance, nor could she chew many foods. Even after speech therapy, her damaged tongue would not allow her to enunciate certain sounds and she had to speak more slowly.

"I had always been a confident person. I was a teacher, a lawyer, and a businesswoman. I just wasn't the same person after the shooting. I didn't work for two years. I had always been this healthy person, and now I had these limitations."

Thompson nodded.

"It affected my family too. My husband had to be my nurse after my surgeries. It was hard on both of my sons to see me go through all of this. My older son wanted to come home from college and felt guilty that he couldn't be home with me. My younger son was in high school and saw me in the hospital and in pain at home. I was on my way to watch him wrestle that evening when I stopped at Burger King. He became convinced that my injuries were all his fault. He reasoned that if I hadn't been in a hurry to go to his match, I wouldn't have stopped at the fast-food restaurant that night. He carried all this guilt with him, something I didn't know at first."

Karin Ho saw something that the others didn't. Thompson's shoulders were shaking, and she sensed that he was about to cry.

"Do you need to take a break, Richard?" Karin asked.

"Yes."

The two stepped out of the conference room together. Once outside the room, he cried noticeably, tears running down his face.

"How do you feel?" Karin asked.

"I feel messed up," he answered. "I hurt everybody in that family."

Frank Malone joined them outside the conference room. He watched as Karin and Thompson talked.

"She's a nice lady. How could I have done this to her?"

"Now you know. It's always better to know, don't you think?" Karin asked.

Thompson did not answer.

"Take as much time as you need. Tell me when you're ready to go back in there, or if you want to stop the session, we can do that too," Karin said.

"No. Just give me another minute. I'll be all right."

A few minutes later, the big man nodded to Karin and told her that he was ready to resume the session. After sitting down again, he looked at Marie. He was composed, and he hoped that no one suspected that he'd cried out of their presence.

"I don't understand why you just don't want to hurt me," he said.

Marie looked away for a moment before reestablishing eye contact with him. "Richard, for many years, I did want to hurt you. I wanted to cause you the same pain that you'd caused me. I wanted to shoot you right through the jaw. I've been struggling with that anger for a long time. I feel like it's gone, and I don't want it to come back. That's a big reason why I'm here to talk to you person to person."

Neither spoke for a while; then Thompson asked, "How are your sons doing now?"

Marie smiled. "They're doing very well now."

Thompson's concern for her sons—and it appeared to be genuine—opened something in Marie. He had shown empathy, and this moved her. A thought began to take hold. *When I think about this more, I will probably forgive him*, she reasoned. Everyone waited for Marie to resume the dialogue, but she continued to just sit there, her face unreadable. *If I am eventually going to forgive him, why don't I just do it now? That will be my gift to him.*

Marie leaned forward in her chair and looked at Thompson and then at her hands. She was not sure how to begin. She made eye contact with him again before she started. "Richard, I did not plan to say this today. I didn't think I would ever say these words to you, but I forgive you."

The room was silent for a few more moments. Marie thought she saw relief in his eyes.

"And you need to forgive yourself," Marie added. Thompson nodded.

There, she'd said it. She felt a peace and a lightness, a relief that she hadn't expected. She hoped that her anger would never return, but she knew that only time would tell.

After that, the conversation wound down quickly. She asked him a few more questions about his job prospects after he was released. He explained that he would be living at home and had the support of his mom and two sisters there. He looked forward to spending time with his daughter, whom he hadn't seen in many years.

Karin Ho said a few concluding remarks, and the participants stood. Marie had one more thing to say. "Richard, would you like to shake hands?"

Richard Thompson looked at Frank Malone, who nodded his permission. He held out his hand, and Marie took it.

EPILOGUE

July 8, 2018

On a Sunday afternoon in July of 2018, I waited to meet Richard Thompson at a Red Robin restaurant in North Olmsted, Ohio, a western suburb of Cleveland. In Marie's papers, she'd found an address for Richard that was at least twenty years old. Using that address, I'd sent him a letter explaining that I was writing a book about Marie and asking if he would talk to me.

After several months had gone by with no response, I'd given up hope that I'd hear from him. Then I had several missed calls on my cell phone from an unidentified caller who hadn't left a voice message. I wondered if the caller might be Richard. Over the next few days, I called the number several times, but no one ever picked up on the other end. On what I had decided would be my final try, Richard Thompson answered my call.

His voice was pleasant, and I detected no edge or anger in it. He apologized for not getting back to me sooner, but he'd had a difficult time deciding what to do after reading my letter.

"I've got a teenage daughter who I'd never told about my time in prison. I wasn't sure I wanted her to find out about it in a book," he explained. "I finally decided to tell her, and after I did, she and her mom both encouraged me to talk to you."

Scheduling a meeting was difficult because Richard didn't have much free time. He worked six days a week and only had Sundays off.

On those Sunday mornings, he always attended church services. I'd offered to drive to his house on a Sunday afternoon, but he'd insisted on meeting me halfway at the Red Robin. We had picked this Sunday, July 8, at 2 p.m.

I'd arrived about ten minutes early and waited for him in the glassed-in vestibule at the restaurant's front entrance. Just before 2 p.m., I saw a large African American man, at least six feet five inches tall and over three hundred pounds, walking toward the door. I was sure this was the fifty-year-old Richard, and I stood to greet him. He was dressed casually in a short-sleeve shirt and gray cotton pants. As I watched him approach, there was something careless and unconcerned in his gait. After introducing myself, I smiled and extended my hand. We both must have been slightly nervous because our handshake did not quite connect; Richard squeezed my fingers before my hand could fully slide into his.

We sat across from each other in a booth and studied our menus. When the waitress arrived, Richard ordered a cheeseburger and curly fries. "Do you still have unlimited seconds on the fries?" he asked. After she confirmed that they did, he told me, "My wife's always on me about my cholesterol, but every now and then, I just want to eat what I want."

I explained again that I was writing a book about Marie and to do that accurately, I wanted to learn more about him and the events of December 11, 1987. "I'd like to record our conversation so I don't miss something you say while I'm taking notes. Is that okay with you?" I asked.

He nodded.

Over the next two hours, we talked about his childhood, his parents and siblings, his high school basketball career, his drug addiction, the robberies he'd committed with Christopher Martin, his arrest, his nine years in prison, and his life since he'd returned home. He never refused to answer a question, even the tough ones that delved into his criminal past and life in prison. As the afternoon wore on, Richard revealed more and more of himself while the waitress replenished his plate with curly fries several times.

Without being boastful, he was proud of how he'd turned his life around after being released from prison. He'd stayed out of trouble with the law. For most of those years, he'd been employed as a machinist, only out of work for a few weeks when his employer closed its shop and he'd had to find a new job. Several weeks after his release, he'd been introduced to the daughter of his mother's best friend. Something had clicked between the two, and they had been married for nineteen years. His wife was a schoolteacher, and their only child, a daughter, was an honor student in high school. He'd also reconnected with the daughter that he'd fathered before he'd gone to prison. At the urging of his mother and wife, he'd returned to the church and had served as a deacon for the past nine years.

I could see that he'd succeeded when many ex-cons had not. "Richard, you've never been in trouble since you were released. Why do you think that is?" I asked.

Richard explained that being separated from his family was the most difficult part of his nine-year incarceration. "Well, you know I had a six-month-old baby daughter when I was locked up. I seen her once when she was four, and then I didn't see her again until I got out. By then, she was ten. My dad died when I was in prison, and I couldn't go to his funeral. I never want to be in that position again. It seemed like nobody visited me."

The nine years in prison had been tough on Richard in other ways. He'd flout a prison rule or get in a fight with another inmate and end up in solitary confinement. "Those first two or three years, I spent a lot of time in the hole. I finally got tired of that and decided that if I wanted to get out of there, I'd have to follow the rules."

Richard explained that as a teenager, he didn't believe that rules applied to him. Because he was a high school basketball star, his teachers and coaches had "let [him] skate" when he'd broken the rules, allowing him to maintain his athletic eligibility. "So I thought I could get away with it outside of school too," he said.

As a teenager, there were things he wanted that his parents couldn't afford. "To get the stuff I wanted, I robbed and sold weed. In prison, I realized that my mom and dad had always made sure I got what I needed, not necessarily all the things I wanted. I understand that now."

"But you also stole to support a drug habit, right?" I asked.

"Yeah, I was getting high all the time. I needed the money for weed and coke. If I hadn't been arrested for what happened at Burger King, I'd probably be dead by now," he said.

As we talked, it became clear that it wasn't just the deterrent effect of prison that had kept him out of trouble after his release. He'd also stayed away from drugs. Once home, he'd joined a local chapter of Narcotics Anonymous, and he'd come under the wing of a tough sponsor. "He helped me stay clean. No doubt about that."

He abruptly changed subjects. "So how is Marie doing?" he asked.

I explained that she was retired and was enjoying life with her husband and family. Her two sons had taken over their father's business, and both lived in the area. They had children, and Marie spent quality time with her grandchildren.

"That's good," he said. "That's really good."

Because the conversation had turned to Marie, I asked, "Can I take you back to the meeting you had with Marie in prison?"

He nodded.

"What do you remember about it?" I asked.

"I didn't know what to expect. She could have slapped me or cussed at me. I just didn't know what she would do. But she was real calm. She spoke to me like the way you and me are talking right now, person to person. She didn't talk down to me. I remember this vividly. I had to call a recess because she made me cry and I didn't want nobody to see me cry."

"I remember hearing about that," I said.

"It seemed like it was just me and her in that room," he continued. "I don't know how to explain it. It was like we was locked in. She was this nice lady with a husband and two sons, and I'd hurt them all. What I done was awful, and she could've hated me for the rest of her life, but instead she forgave me. It was a huge weight off my shoulders."

Richard was expressing the same feelings that Marie had also described. In the warden's conference room, they had both been a part of something extremely powerful, and it had changed them. Others in the room had felt it too.

As our meeting broke up, Richard asked me to say hello to Marie for him. I promised him that I would give her a full report.

✿ ✿ ✿

The next day, I called Marie, who was very interested in my meeting with Richard.

"I haven't seen him in twenty years," she said. "You know, I met with Richard one more time after the prison visit. I asked Richard's parole officer if Richard would agree to another meeting, this time at the parole office. I was really curious as to how he was doing. I also hoped that if we met outside the prison, we'd be on an equal footing."

"What happened?" I asked.

"Richard agreed to the second meeting and brought his fiancée with him. I was really pleased that he had a job and was doing well. We had a very cordial conversation, but we never met again."

As I told her about the meeting, Marie seemed both relieved and excited about Richard's continued success since leaving prison. She quizzed me for about a half an hour, squeezing from me as much as I could remember about the visit.

"I'm so glad he's doing well," she said.

"We also talked about your prison visit," I said.

"Uh-huh," Marie said expectantly.

"He said the meeting was very important to him. He will never forget your words of forgiveness. They freed him from a burden he'd been carrying for a long time. He didn't realize its weight until it was gone. You really helped him get a fresh start when he got home."

Marie didn't respond for a few seconds, and I pictured her remembering that pivotal moment with Richard. "That meeting was very important to me as well," she began. "I was surprised that my anger and fear never returned. On the drive home from the prison, I felt elated. I knew that feeling would eventually fade, and it did. However, it was replaced by something more sustainable but just as powerful. Despite all the bad things that had happened to me, I hoped that Richard would have a good life going forward. And that feeling has never left me."

After Marie and I said our good-byes, I thought about Marie's journey. She had won "victories" in both the criminal and civil cases, yet she had not been made whole by them—the avowed purpose of the civil justice system. She did not find peace until she took further steps herself. Her story reinforces the unfortunate truth that the legal system can only carry a person so far.

It was only after Marie and Richard talked about what had happened that she was able to gain a meaningful closure and heal emotionally. Something had been missing for Richard too. Although he'd completed his prison term and theoretically paid his debt to society, without that meeting, his future would still have been troubled by his past. Their conversation led to forgiveness and the opportunity for a fresh start.

As it turned out, compassion and understanding were liberating for both of them.